I Will Fear No Evil

*True stories of
faith from those who
have walked "through the valley"*

C. A. Murray

Pacific Press® Publishing Association
Nampa, Idaho
Oshawa, Ontario, Canada

Edited by B. Russell Holt
Designed by Michelle C. Petz
Cover photo © Shunsuke Yamamoto / Photonica
Cover photo digital enhancements by Michelle C. Petz

Copyright © 2001 by
Pacific Press® Publishing Association
Printed in the United States of America
All Rights Reserved

THE AUTHOR ASSUMES RESPONSIBILITY
FOR THE ACCURACY OF ALL FACTS AND
QUOTATIONS CITED IN THIS BOOK

Library of Congress Cataloging-in-Publication Data

Murray, C. A. (Clement A.), 1950-
   I will fear no evil: true stories of those who've walked through the valley / C. A. Murry.
     p. cm.
   ISBN 0-8163-1808-5
    1. City Churches. 2. City Churches—New York (State)—New York—Case studies. 3. Seventh-day Adventists—New York (State)—New York—Biography. 4. New York (N. Y.)—Church History—20th century. I. Title.

BV637 .M847 2001
253'.09747'1—dc21   00-062397

CONTENTS

Dedication 4

Foreword 5

Preface 6

A Note to the Reader 7

Chapter One .... *The Initiation* 9

Chapter Two .... *Delissa* 15

Chapter Three .... *Tamara* 38

Chapter Four .... *Juliet* 66

Chapter Five .... *Simon Says* 82

Chapter Six .... *Ministering to the Fallen* 91

Chapter Seven .... *Stopping the Fall* 100

Chapter Eight .... *The Land of No Regrets* 112

Epilogue 120

A Conversation With C. A. Murry 121

Dedication

This book is dedicated to the countless fighters who, having enlisted in the army of Christ, fight each day for their lives. To those persons, plain and simple, unstoried and unheralded—those multiplied small fish who swim in very large ponds, who live and love and fight and die, and who in their own quiet way, carry the banner for all of those who refuse to let the lords of this world defeat them.

And to all those who have found the secret of winning and losing. Those who every day prove that the strongest force in the universe is the power of love. Those living "saints" who understand that a fusion of the Infinite with the finite guarantees success. Those who have come to understand that, love Him or not, believe in Him or not, accept Him or not, above all and beneath all, around all, and in all—there is God.

To Gwendolyn, Donna, Irma, Kevin, Becky and Danny, Mona, Lee Anna, Hamp, Luiu O, Delbert, Whintley Holbrook and family, Esmeé, and Larry.

Thanks, Ben Carson, for your encouragement. Thank you, Lady J, for the housekeeping. Special thanks to my partner and chief diagnostician, Yvonne Lewis. Thanks, Gloria Felder, for your nimble fingers. A world of thanks to you, Booboo.

Thanks, Stennett Trevor and Walter Arties, for being courageous and trusting. Thanks, Fred D. Willis, for so many years ago.

Foreword

The stories in this book are all quite true. Admittedly, one or two ancillary details have been altered. The names have certainly been changed, and in one instance, the city in which the principals reside has been changed. Any additional alterations are on that same modest scale.

The dialogue, situations, and events are all as true and real and accurate as memory can recall them. Nothing has been invented, embellished, or added. Some of what was fairly graphic conversation has been somewhat sanitized. What you will read is the truth, the whole truth, and nothing but the truth.

I should like to add that these events portray themselves every day in the city. For the urban dweller, both Christian and non-Christian, these things constitute the facts of life. They do not go away because we come to Christ.

The Christian community cannot bury its head in ecclesiastical sand and pretend that these things are not out there. They are. And, as I hope to impress upon you, they are here—in our homes, our churches, our businesses. They are right here where we are, and like it or not, believe it or not, accept it or not, they are, in all their terror, very, very real.

Preface

This book holds the distinction of being rejected by three notable publishing houses. Two of the editors from these houses took the time to include a special letter with their notice. I want to thank them.

In both instances, the editors stated that the stories were impelling and moving, that they were well written, and that the book was a commendable first effort, worthy of promotion. However, the fact that I was a first-time author, coupled with the current economic climate, scared them a little. Additionally, neither company was comfortable with material of a religious nature and so, ultimately, both decided against publication.

I was also called in to meet with the CEO of both companies. They encouraged me to keep plugging and not to give up. The head of one of the companies, a large nation-wide publishing house based in Westchester County, New York, gave me his unlisted home telephone number and asked me to call him first should I ever write a nonreligious work.

The third publisher agreed that the material was indeed compelling and that the stories were of great import. Notwithstanding, the editors objected to the "sad nature of the book," and so rejected it for its lack of what was termed "positive take away." They felt that life stories should always end on a positive, upbeat note. To that I must respectfully reply, "Rubbish!"

Real life has its ups and downs, its mountains and valleys. In real life people get wounded. They get hurt, and, yes, they do die. Real life is not a cartoon nor a thirty-minute sitcom nor a fairy tale. Sometimes things work out well; often they do not. Life is not a bowl of cherries. That is why we have, and need, Jesus. Any life that ends in the arms of Jesus must be considered a victorious life.

Whether the life be long or short, troublesome or carefree, if an individual dies "saved" in Christ, he or she has not lost, but won—and that is cause for cosmic celebration. Those who stand by Jesus and live with Jesus and die with Jesus will live forever. That, my friends, is the ultimate "positive take away."

"Death in Christ is not such a bad thing,
Better to die in Jesus than to live without Him."

A Note to the Reader

Throughout the pages of this book you will notice references to the Sabbath, particularly to services held, sermons preached, and meetings convened on the Sabbath. This is occasioned by the fact that I am a Seventh-day Adventist minister.

Principal among the doctrinal beliefs of my church is the observance of the seventh-day Sabbath in accordance with the fourth of the Ten Commandments found, among other places, in Exodus 20:8-11.

Many believe and preach that the Sabbath was changed from Saturday to Sunday by, during, or after Christ. This is a position for which there is no biblical basis. Not only were the commandments not changed by Jesus, but indeed, He spent His life fulfilling them and giving them pragmatic vitality (see Matthew 5:17-48).

Consequently, Seventh-day Adventists continue to worship on the Sabbath in accordance with the Lord's wishes, stated not only to the Jews, but instituted at Creation when the Lord ceased His creative activity and rested on the seventh day. This He did, not because He was tired but, to give us an example for all time. He said, *"Remember the Sabbath day to keep it holy."* That is what I, and nearly eleven million Seventh-day Adventists worldwide, endeavor to do.

I Will Fear No Evil

CHAPTER ONE

The Initiation

I was born and reared in Buffalo, New York, the second largest city in the state of New York, and considered myself a fairly sophisticated urban dweller. I arrived in New York City in June 1974. I assumed that I was "ready" for New York. After all, I had visited it on at least three occasions. I knew Brooklyn from the Bronx and Manhattan from Queens. "Pretty good," I thought.

I soon came to realize that no other city can completely prepare you for life in New York City. There is nothing to equal New York City. Not in the state, not in the country, not in the world. Nothing can adequately prepare you for living here—short of living here. The traffic, the noise, the crime, the crush of people, the incessant activity, and the sheer pace of the city are intoxicating and, I might add, addictive.

My initiation came one day shortly after my arrival. I made my way across the Manhattan Bridge from Brooklyn to Canal Street bordering Chinatown in Manhattan and proceeded north through the section of town called the "Bowery." I stopped at an intersection, and from nowhere an army of disheveled men appeared. They made their way to the waiting automobiles. The men were unshaven. Their clothes were soiled, and many were shoeless.

Due to my intent staring, I initially failed to see the man standing near my own car door. As my eyes fell on him, I was surprised to see how young he was and the sadness etched on his face. Our eyes met, and we stared blankly at each other for a few moments. He broke off his gaze and spat a mixture of saliva and thick, greenish-yellow phlegm on my windshield. He smeared it with a tattered, filthy sleeve and held out his hand for a tip.

I was stunned beyond reason. In my young life, I had nothing to compare this incident to. I sat dumbfounded for a few seconds. His eyes again met mine as I reached into my pocket and gave him a dollar. I could not believe what had just happened.

The irritated honking of the drivers behind me shocked me to my senses. I pulled away, pumping my windshield washer furiously as I turned on the wipers. They moved slowly in a futile effort to remove the viscous fluid, but succeeded only in smearing it further. I pumped washer fluid until my reservoir was drained. It wasn't working. I was forced into the realization that this would have to be cleaned by hand—*my* hand! "Welcome to the Big Apple!" I thought.

I must admit that in the ensuing years I have become somewhat jaded. I have learned to cope with the almost endless numbers of windshield washers that lurk at hundreds of key intersections all over the city. Most are far better equipped now than my inaugural friend of 1974. Armed with spray bottles, towels, cloths, and squeegees, many are quite efficient (and others annoying). Now only the finest windshield washers merit even fifty of my hard-earned cents. (I pay considerably less for spit!)

Perhaps New York City should be described as a mission field. Though located in North America, it can at times be as primitive and savage as the deepest jungle or remotest outback. It can be merciless for those who are unprepared to meet and deal with it. It

THE INITIATION

forces you to abandon wide-eyed innocence in favor of wary cynicism—the safer, more appropriate attitude of street-wise people.

New Yorkers learn to give their love and trust grudgingly. Some sleep, literally, with one eye open. Most have at least one story recounting a fraud or scam perpetrated on themselves or someone they know. New Yorkers rarely relax mentally, as such a lapse could prove hazardous to their health. Free time spent in a park or at the beach merely provides another opportunity for the unsuspecting to get taken. Consequently, an in-the-know resident of "Gotham" is always on guard.

One might think this reason enough for a mass exodus from the city. Though it is true that New York City does lose appreciable numbers of residents each year, it also accepts many new ones. There are large numbers of people who are most passionate about living here and who could not conceive of living elsewhere.

New York is a city that never sleeps and rarely slows down. It incessantly moves, shakes, flexes itself. It is truly a marvel, and yet there is a price to pay. Crime is high and perhaps more prevalent here than any other place on planet Earth. The people of New York City have learned to live by the creed, "Look out for Number One." Translation: "Take care of yourself, first, last, and always."

There are in the neighborhood of eighty-five Seventh-day Adventist churches in New York City with approximately 30,000 members, but we still remain a drop in a very large and secularized bucket that contains every sort of amusement and vice to titillate and occupy the worldly mind and to beckon and distract the religious. Opera, theaters, museums, Wall Street, the stock exchange, art galleries, and foods from the ends of the earth—all these are part of the rich culture of the city. But sadly, there is another side to New York City, the side revealed by the statistics.

New York City houses more than 475,000 drug addicts. It has well over 250,000 homeless men, women, and children. It is one of

I WILL FEAR NO EVIL

the three world epicenters of the AIDS epidemic. It is home to some of the most brazen and aggressive prostitutes on planet Earth. These prostitutes don't wait to be propositioned, but are indeed quite comfortable coming over to your car to initiate and close the deal. New York averages just short of 2,000 homicides a year; it is consistently near the top among U.S. cities in that disturbing category.

It's a city that sees thousands of children born not unlike the one I met in 1989, drug addicted and shaking violently. The poor child, who lived only five days, never slept and never stopped shaking until he closed his eyes in death. The nurses would not name him or even handle him.

"We knew we couldn't save this one," the charge nurse told me. "He never had a chance, so we stayed away. We didn't want to love him. It just hurts too much when we lose them. When you love them and they die on you, they take a little slice of your heart, so we try to hold back for the sake of our own sanity. But it doesn't always work."

I understood her words well, for I had developed a love for this little shaking child. I had, against her counsel, visited him on three of the five days of his life, and when he died, he took a bit of my soul with him. I was informed that once these unclaimed and unwanted children die, their bodies are used by medical students for surgical practice and organ identification. Otherwise, they are incinerated.

It is not that other cities are not plagued with these problems. It is simply that New York City has so much more. Everything in New York City is multiplied. What other cities have by the tens, New York has by the hundreds or thousands. If it is bad in City A, then it is quadrupled in New York City. The vices and sins kept underground in other municipalities openly flaunt themselves in New York City. There is much fear here. The average apartment

THE INITIATION

door in New York City holds no less than three separate locks. Often they carry as many as five or six.

Often, when I've visited church members and announced who I was (no New York City dweller would ever open a door without making absolutely sure who is on the other side), I have waited patiently as the person systematically unchained and unclasped, unbolted, unbarred, unlocked, and disarmed the array of devices designed to prevent unwanted intrusion. In New York City homes and apartments, the "peephole" is obligatory. The song, "New York, New York," sung by Frank Sinatra, intones, "If I can make it there, I'll make it anywhere. . . ." It has long been held that if one can pastor successfully in New York City, he can pastor anywhere. Perhaps that is partially true, because the city is home to people from everywhere. There is no continent, no country, no ethnicity that is not represented by the thousands in New York City. It is true: if one can succeed in New York City, the odds are that he has enough to make it in any town. And it is certainly true that if one can drive in New York City, he is more than a match for any municipality in the civilized world—or in the uncivilized world, for that matter.

After twenty-six years in this town, I must admit that there is also incredible beauty here. There are wonders and sights to be found here that are found no where else. The Lord has not left this city destitute of kindness.

There is an aggressive, almost militant, religious community here that is determined to help improve the quality of life in this city. I have been blessed to witness growing out of the mud of New York City, Christian lilies that have exhibited faith equal to that found and practiced in Scripture.

In the past five years, I have had three church members lose members of their families to murder by gunshot. Two of the three crimes remain unsolved, and yet in each of the cases, the faith and love for Christ possessed by the surviving family members is aston-

I WILL FEAR NO EVIL

ishing. Over and over, when confronted and challenged, the power of Christ has pushed back the forces of darkness, and those assailed by the enemy have stood in heaven's strength and have won victory in Jesus.

This, then, is the backdrop for the stories of three women who walked into and passed out of my life and who have left an impression that will remain with me forever. Truly they were angels, women whose lives were dedicated to Christ. Women who took all that Satan had to give and fought back valiantly—and who, in losing, won! Their courage and strength are exemplary. I have no doubt but that as you meet them, you, too, will find and hold them deep within your heart.

I have been privileged to meet many luminaries in today's world, men and women who are considered prominent—Jimmy Carter, Desmond Tutu, Whitney Houston, Dionne Warwick, Stephanie Mills, Roberta Flack, Mario Cuomo, Paul Simon, Muhammed Ali, Sugar Ray Leonard, George Lukas, and Clifton Davis. None of these have impressed me as have the three women whose stories follow. The brilliance of these prominent people, these "stars," pales in the light that shines from the lives of these "fallen angels." It occurs to me that the thing that sets someone apart is not his or her vocation or natural talent to sing or act or play sports. The true arbiter of one's greatness is character. Someone once said, "Our capital (currency) is our character." A rich person, a famous person, a talented person with no character is worthless. Character cannot be purchased; it is forged in the crucible of life. Character is so terribly needed in our world today.

I Will Fear No Evil

CHAPTER TWO

Delissa

"I JUST DON'T WANT TO BE SICK"

To this day there are only a half dozen or so persons who know all of this story. I was sworn never to tell the story while she lived. She asked and received from me a promise that no matter what transpired, I was to share her confidence with no one until after her passing. Though I was severely tested, it was a promise that I kept.

Chronologically, this story is not the first of those I have to tell. But I have chosen to place it so because of the impact that Delissa had on me. It was in reflecting on her that I was driven to begin and complete this book.

I remember well the Sabbath it all began. I had just completed the morning sermon and was in my study preparing my mind and my stomach for an eagerly anticipated lunch. I rarely eat anything of consequence on mornings when I am scheduled to preach. It was then that a deaconess came to my study to ask me to visit Delissa.

Deaconesses are an elected group of female church members, usually older women, who act as "mothers" in the church. Most have been members for many years and have gained the trust and confidence of the membership. Consequently, they are privy to more secret and personal information than most church members. Sometimes they know more than the pastor. If you want to know anything about anybody, ask a deaconess.

"She wants to see you and Elder Roberts, please pastor," the deaconess importuned. "Go now!" When a deaconess speaks using that tone—the kind that puts you in mind of your mother telling you to wash behind your ears—the statement at first glance may seem to be a request, but lying just beneath the request is an urgency that lets you know it is really an order. When little old ladies give such orders, you listen. And if you are smart, you follow them. I sensed the urgency in her voice and decided to skip lunch.

We drove the fifteen blocks to Delissa's apartment building. I knew where the building was. She had been one of the first members I had visited after assuming this pastorate. She had custody of her granddaughter whom we had baptized, and she was giving Bible studies to the neighbor across the hall. Although having only minimal formal education, Delissa read the Bible voraciously and was an aggressive witness for her faith. When she wanted to study the Bible with you, you either said, "Yes," or she nagged you until you did. That was the word around the apartment building.

I'm not sure what the term "model Christian" means, but if indeed such persons exist, Delissa would have to be numbered among them. A committed, sincere, and deeply spiritual woman, she was caring, supportive, quick to volunteer, and eager to witness for her faith. Delissa consistently arrived at prayer meeting thirty minutes before it began. She testified every Wednesday night at the midweek service, and always her simple words were upbeat and joyous, full of praise and thanksgiving. Rarely did she ever speak of problems in her life; her testimonies were always seasoned with hope. She joyfully dove into fund-raising campaigns and literature distribution schemes. She had little love for the politics of the church or holding office. She was content to serve Christ in the pew and in the streets and on her job. She was the kind of member that pastors love to have.

Delissa was part of a little group of women who brought their lunches to church on Sabbath. As did a number of similar groups, they would sit together at a table in the rear of the fellowship hall, eat their sandwiches, nuts, and cookies, discuss the sermon, the Bible, or the Sabbath School lesson, and just enjoy themselves in the Lord. Their fare rarely varied—sandwiches, nuts, fruits, cookies or homemade cake, and the obligatory bottle of 7-Up or ginger ale. I came to understand that the food was secondary. What counted was the friendship, the fellowship, and the weekly class reunion of friends who shared a deep and abiding love for each other. In many cases this love bound them with ties closer than those that connected them to their biological siblings.

There is an intimate fraternity among Christians that makes little sense to the outside world. But to those involved it is real and sweet and satisfying. It was this love, this caring, that was nurtured and affirmed at these tables each week—friends being friendly with friends. Part of my weekly after-sermon ritual was to make the rounds to each of these tables. Each little "cell" had different foods and conversation, and I looked forward to these times.

I also quickly learned that the ladies in these groups liked it when I bummed a little food from them. So each Sabbath, as I came and fellowshipped I would "borrow" a cookie or some nuts or fruit. The response to those times when I tried to refuse the offering let me know that these ladies (and some men) enjoyed feeding their pastor, and I enjoyed their fellowship and love.

Delissa was at the center of one of these groups, and I enjoyed stopping by her table. I recall teasing her one Sabbath for gaining a little weight and suggesting that I take some extra cookies for her sake. She quickly responded that she did not need the weight, but neither did I and that she would find some slim person to give them to.

I WILL FEAR NO EVIL

Her joy was infectious. She enjoyed a good joke and could trade puns with the best. Rarely did she come up short when it came to exchanging wisecracks, and yet this facet of her complex character was rarely viewed by those outside the circle of her closest friends.

To the outside world she was a pious, shy, almost retiring woman, not given to initiating conversation and answering only those questions asked. Though hesitant to speak out on most subjects, there were two times when she spoke freely and unencumbered. One such time was the Wednesday night prayer meeting service when the opportunity was extended to give testimony as to the blessings of the Lord. Delissa underwent an amazing metamorphosis during these seasons. The shy, halting speaker became a passionate, convincing, convicting, eloquent apologist for her faith. The second could be witnessed at the table on Sabbaths when these women, in their forties and fifties, gathered to eat, talk, and exchange the occasional quip. Their conversation was nonstop and animated; they were like high-school girls discussing their dates. To see Delissa at these times was to see happiness unabated. Most of these women wore hats to church, but in the fellowship hall it was time for hats to come off and hair to come down (sometimes shoes came off, too).

So I was not prepared for the joyless, terror-stricken face that greeted me in the shadowy apartment that Sabbath afternoon when I, with Elder Roberts, followed my deaconess's urging. It was a bright, sunny, April afternoon, but Delissa's apartment was darkened. The shades were drawn, and a solitary lamp burned in the living room.

I uttered a silent prayer, we entered and sat down. I knew the news would not be good. Life would really have to have delivered one of its hardest, cruelest blows to get this lady down. It was not in her nature to be morose.

Few times in my life have I heard the kind of wail that came

DELISSA

from the very depths of that woman's being. I felt a chill course from my feet to the hairs of my head. I had never heard a sound so pitiful, and it left me cold and apprehensive. Her husband, sitting cross-legged in a chair on the opposite side of the room, rocked back and forth. Her cry seemed to noticeably unsettle him. My eyes turned to him for a moment. I had seen him only once before and then just for a few minutes. He was a handsome man with sharp, distinguished features and wavy hair streaked with gray. I also saw something that disturbed me; I couldn't quite put my finger on it, but something was wrong. He was handsome, but . . . .

Delissa began to speak. "A few years ago my husband and I ran into some difficulties. We weren't 'getting on' so well." I had heard the term used before. "Getting on" is a term that is used in some cultures almost exclusively in the family setting. It is used in reference to relationships between children and parents, between siblings, but most often in describing the relationship between a husband and wife. When a husband and wife are "not getting on well," it can mean anything from not speaking to each other to not sleeping together to outright abuse.

"He was with other women," Delissa continued. "I didn't know. I never kept track of these things. I didn't follow him. I didn't know that there were other women in his life. He wasn't living at home at that time. We were apart. I wasn't with anyone. A few months ago he got sick—very, very sick. His fever was high, and he lost a lot of weight. The doctor said it looked like AIDS. They ran tests, and it was true. I couldn't believe my ears. I couldn't believe it was true," she said, shaking her head before burying it in her hands.

I looked at her husband who was staring intently at a picture of Christ on the opposite wall. He began to sway in his seat as though each word carried the force of a boxer's jab. The pain he was feeling was not physical, but it was nonetheless real.

"I couldn't believe it," Delissa blurted out. "AIDS was something that other people had. You hear about it on the radio or read about it in the papers, but you never think . . . ." Her words were cut short by a deep sigh from her husband. His face bore the impress of a man carrying the weight of the world.

Delissa collected herself and continued. "I hadn't been feeling too well recently and went for a check-up. The doctor said I should be tested, too. I took the test, but I just knew I didn't have AIDS. The results came back yesterday. They told me I have it. I have this thing." She brushed her arms furiously, as though the virus was on her sleeves, and sank down dejectedly on the living room floor.

She sobbed uncontrollably for a minute, but then forced herself to regroup. "I don't know why; I don't know why" she said.

"I didn't know. I just didn't know," her husband interrupted, as if defending himself. "I would have never brought that back. I never wanted to hurt her." His sad eyes filled with tears as his words were choked off by a coughing spell. He was thin and somewhat frail and shook violently with each cough. I walked over and lifted Delissa from the floor. She was a full-figured woman of about 170 pounds. Her buckling knees threw the bulk of her weight on me, causing me to lose balance momentarily.

Once seated on the couch, she continued, "Am I going to die? I am going to die." Her question and answer came in rapid succession. "What should I do?" she said, turning her reddened eyes to me.

"You ought to trust Jesus," I said. "What else can you do? You honor Him. You love Him. I've heard you say so on many occasions. Now you will have to cash in on that trust. You have been given one of the heaviest burdens that anyone can carry. I won't insult you by saying, 'I know how you feel.' All I know is that Jesus knows, and I know that you know Him. You must put this in His hands and rest in Him.

She was calmer now. Her tears were dried. "We don't know

what heaven's disposition will be on this," I continued. "We must put it in His hands."

"Yes," her husband chimed in. "You're a Christian, a good Christian. Just pray with the pastor, and Jesus will heal you." His words surprised, disturbed, and upset me. I realized that although they echoed the teaching of many of the popular preachers of the day, they were far from the truth. I knew that Jesus was no pocket magician to be called upon when you need a quick miracle or a health fix. God says Yes, and He says No. He determines which response is appropriate. The how, the why, the when, indeed, the if is all in the hands of a God of love.

Delissa's husband was not a Christian. I had never seen him in church. To my knowledge, he had never professed a belief in Jesus. Later that day he would promise to begin attending church. His words did not impress me as the product of a genuine faith or conversion experience. My skepticism was justified. To my knowledge, he never set foot in any church, and his funeral was not a religious ceremony. I saw his statement as an attempt to discharge a load of guilt that was crushing his spirit. I wished his statement that Jesus would heal his wife were true; I wished that we could wave a magic wand or snap our fingers and change these things—heal her and free him of the guilt that for him was worse than AIDS. Oh, how I wished, but this was real life, and wishes don't often come true in real life. This situation needed more than a single wish—much more!

Sitting there on the couch, I could almost hear Delissa's heart pounding. Her breathing was slow, deep, and measured, as she attempted to maintain a semblance of composure. The air was thick and heavy, and the darkness only added to the gloom and despair resident in the room. She was sinking before my eyes. I felt impelled to change the mood slightly. "Tell me about Jesus," I said. She appeared momentarily to be surprised, as the request seemed to come from left field.

Delissa closed her eyes, drifting off in thought. She began to speak of her childhood—the tough times, her lack of extensive formal education, how Christ had blessed her, brought her to America, and given her a solid, stable, if not exorbitantly high-paying job. She spoke of giving Him her new life and the joy she felt, the friends she had made, and the peace she had in loving Jesus.

"Has He abandoned you?" I asked. I was met with silence. She sat up, her eyes focused squarely on mine. A puzzled look crossed her face. I found myself wondering if that look was a response to my question or a self-questioning of her relationship with her Lord. I soon had my answer.

"This is not His fault; Jesus is my Friend," she said with a resolve that came from her soul. She sounded like a teenager defending her closest girlfriend. "He would never leave me." Her statement ended with a smile that was mirrored in my face.

"Good!" I said. "We don't know what the Lord will do. You must maintain your confidence in Him. Come what may, you must trust Him."

It was on the heels of these remarks that Delissa made a statement she would repeat to me a number of times on that day and over the ensuing months. "I'm not afraid of death. I don't care if I die," she asserted. "It doesn't matter; I just don't want to be sick. I don't want to waste away and be sick. I'm afraid to be sick."

Delissa, I discovered, was one of those fortunate few who had never been really sick in her life. Except for a few childhood diseases and an occasional cold as an adult, she was unfamiliar with sickness on a personal level. She was a robust, healthy woman who, by her own admission, was carrying about twenty excess pounds. Most germs didn't have a chance to assault her. She ate healthy foods, kept herself well covered in cold weather, walked incessantly, and, except for an occasional cake and ice cream binge, lived a healthy, conscientious life. She drank eight glasses of water every day. Her

DELISSA

skin was blemish-free and bright. One just couldn't envision Delissa sick.

Her faith, though strong, would be tested. The thought that she would be reduced to a helpless weakling terrified her. The weeks and months of slow decline were something she dreaded. She had an example of what to expect. It was sitting directly across from her in the person of her husband. He had lost over fifty pounds, and the array of medicine bottles with his name on each label was staggering. He had already been taken to the hospital on three separate occasions. Fever had racked his body, and he had infections the name of which neither Delissa nor he could pronounce. This was the eventuality she so feared.

Each day she was forced to look at what was to be her future. A slow, stealthy decline, an inexorable march to the grave, marked by pain and loneliness and saddled with the additional weight of a social stigma to which even church members were not immune.

"I don't want to be sick," she repeated. "I don't mind dying, if that's what must happen, but not sick. Please, God, not sick," she said, looking heavenward.

As we spoke, I learned that she also feared that if her fellow church members knew of her condition, she would be stared at, talked about, and shunned. This was a fear from which she was never released. A sad commentary, I thought, on the Christian community, that a person who is HIV positive has the additional burden and fear that if church members were to find out, he or she would be shunned and in some cases, summarily rejected or talked of and whispered about and steered clear of. It was at this point that Delissa swore me to the reluctant secrecy which was to last as long as she lived.

"I am going to take care of my husband. I promised to. I promised God. If killing would change things . . . ." She stopped abruptly, catching the sense of what she was saying. "I'll take care of him; he is still my husband," she affirmed.

Her eyes searched mine, asking a question I could not decipher. They shifted to her now sobbing husband. I followed her glance, staring intently into her face. I looked closely for an evidence of hatred or malice as she looked at her husband. I honestly expected it. Who wouldn't have? I had listened to her charitable words of love and continuing devotion, but I assumed that her face would speak otherwise. As a pastor and counselor, I had learned to listen intently to the words, but also learned that words tell only part of the story. The other, sometimes equally-important part, is told in the face and body language. In most instances these all agree, but often they do not. The words say one thing, the body language another. At that point, the task is to decide which is telling the truth.

Delissa fixed her eyes on her husband. Her gaze seemed cold and hard for a moment, but the icy glare was soon replaced by a soft, pitiful look, the kind one would give to a wounded puppy or to a child who had just fallen and skinned his knee. She appeared momentarily to lose sight of herself as she focused on him. Her words dug into me, and I marveled at a woman who just twenty-four hours earlier had been given the news that her husband had literally signed her death warrant, and who was now planning to care for his needs as long as her health allowed. No anger, no cursing, no swearing or finger pointing. She vowed that hour to stay with him, to stand by him, to care for him, as her God would strengthen her. In that moment, in the face of Delissa I saw Jesus—His love, His grace, and His glory—as I had never seen Him before. My heart was touched, and I knew I was sitting in the presence of an angel. As a true child of God, she was stable and resolute, and she meant what she was saying.

She must have been taken aback by my startled reaction. I stared at her in amazement; her eyes, her nose, her lips. Her face at

DELISSA

that instant was radiating a love that only an indwelling Jesus can generate. I wanted to shout, to scream, to embrace this saint who was showing me what it meant to know Christ. The feeling that gripped me then, and has remained with me to this day, is impossible to describe. In my shoes I curled my toes. I bit my lip and squeezed the sofa and listened to the sermon that Delissa was preaching to her pastor. And yet something in me wanted to cry and weep for this lovely, lonely lady whose courage was breathtaking. I had never met anyone like her, and for a moment I was nonplussed.

Could my ears be hearing correctly? We were in New York City in the late 1980s. A city where people kill one another for looking at them the wrong way. A city where a passenger on the subway was stabbed to death because he neglected to cover his mouth when he sneezed. A city where a man was clubbed to death for touching someone's Mercedes. A city where a woman was raped and then forced to jump from the roof of the eighteen-story apartment building she had been dragged onto. A city where life is bought and sold cheaply. Yet here was Delissa affirming love and life in this city, in the face of death. She had just taken Satan's "Sunday punch" and was still standing strong in the Lord.

I wanted to pray right then, right there, right away—to ratify and seal this moment with prayer. It was time. No more talk, no more useless multiplication of words, no more moth-eaten ministerial platitudes. Prayer! We had to talk to Jesus now. I thanked the Lord for Delissa's courage and strength and asked Jesus to seal her dedication and keep her. I listened to her ask Jesus to bless her husband, her pastor, her friends, and to forgive her for doubting His love. We concluded our prayer, exchanged a few words, and said Goodbye.

I closed the door and walked down the stairs. My mind raced and seethed; the emotional mix boggled me. I was profoundly saddened, yet I had seen Jesus, or as much of Him as I had ever seen in one person. As I sat in my car too stunned to drive, her words repeated themselves in my ears: "I will stay with him. I will care for him because I promised God." I thought about all the responses that Delissa could have had—anger, hate, recrimination—but I saw none of these. I saw someone content with the will of God. She was at peace with Him in the face of this terrible storm.

I put my head on the steering wheel and let the tears flow. And when they were dried, I closed my eyes and begged God to save her. "Faith like that," I told my Lord, "has to be vindicated." I wasn't asking God for healing, not at that instant. Oddly, at that moment physical healing was not on my mind. I was asking God to save her soul and to give her an eternal heavenly home. I wanted her ultimate salvation. To my mind, if anyone deserved heaven, Delissa did. "You must save her, Jesus," I implored.

Winter had passed, and the smell of spring was heavy in the air. All around, nature was calling her creation to life. But in the concrete jungle of New York City, death is never far away. I reflected on the large number of funerals I had been called to conduct since assuming this pastorate. Young, old, gunshot victims, stroke victims, cancer patients, auto fatalities, seven children who were lost in a fire, suicide victims.

During the past five years I had preached at some 110 funerals. I was averaging twenty to twenty-four a year, or one every eighteen days or so. Even with funerals happening that often, I never became immune to the pain. It never became routine. Sure, there were some that touched me more than others; some that hurt personally more than others. But each time I donned my black robe and stood before a grieving family, I was keenly aware of what it means to lose someone you love. The sense of loss and loneliness is always there. I determined in my heart that Delissa would not be alone. She would have my presence and support whenever she needed it.

DELISSA

As I started my car, the noise of the engine startled an animal from the depths of the trash heap near the curb. It scurried quickly across the sidewalk and under the abandoned building adjacent to Delissa's. It was either a fairly small cat or a fairly large rat. Although this was a neighborhood that frightened me somewhat, it occurred to me that this animal and I would probably see a lot of each other over the next several months.

Delissa remained faithful, missing only an occasional church service. She rarely spent the entire day in church, as had been her custom, but her greetings were always seasoned with positive comments, and she maintained a cheerful disposition.

I recall a chance visit to her apartment some months later. Finding the door slightly ajar and fearing the worst, I quickly entered. The smell of pine disinfectant was strong in the air. I found her in the kitchen on her knees, weeping as she cleaned vomit from the linoleum. Thinking that she had taken ill, I asked how she was feeling. "Oh, I'm fine," she said. "My husband got sick, and I'm cleaning it up. I have to do the bedroom and bathroom too."

I asked why the tears. And, sitting in a chair, she explained, "I'm no Christian. I am not what Jesus wants. Sometimes I get mad; sometimes I hate my husband's voice. When I bring him his juice or his medicine, he says, 'Thanks, Babydoll.' He's always called me 'Babydoll,' but I don't like it anymore. I don't want him to call me 'Babydoll' anymore. When he says it now, something starts inside me. Hate builds up. I know that hate doesn't come from Jesus. I want Christ to forgive me and love me and I must love and forgive . . . but it's so hard." Her words choked off by a sob. She dropped again to her knees and resumed her cleaning. A moan from the bedroom was responded to quickly as she excused herself and hurried to her husband. I refused to be impressed or astounded. Delissa had thrown so many curves at me. She had so often bowled me over with her determined, childlike faith that I simply would not allow

I WILL FEAR NO EVIL

myself to be further impressed, and yet I was impressed. She was punishing herself for experiencing a natural response to the most trying of situations. She was on her knees cleaning her husband's vomit, stopping just long enough to rush to his bedside when he moaned. And all the while she was mentally flagellating herself for feeling the slightest bit of resentment or anger at the situation he had brought upon them both.

Truthfully, I didn't know what to expect from her. After dealing so long with humanity's failings and shortcomings (including my own), this glimpse of near perfection was a little difficult to take. It was forcing me to ask myself, "Would I be this charitable? Could I do this?" I was less than anxious to hear my answer. We prayed again and found something to laugh about. I stopped in to see the now-sleeping husband and left. It was early evening, and I wondered if my "friend" was in the trash heap again. I inspected it from a safe distance and determined that he was otherwise engaged.

Delissa's health failed a bit; she wasn't always at her best physically, but her spirits remained high. She did lose some weight, but rather than hurt her appearance, it enhanced it. The twelve to fifteen pounds she dropped improved her looks. A number of people noticed and commented on how well she looked at the new weight. As was her habit, she took the comments humbly, meekly giving credit to the Lord.

In July during a visit to my study, she repeated, "I'm ready to die. I've given all to Jesus. I just don't want to be sick. I am not praying to be healed; just that whatever His will is I will be found doing it."

"May I hug you?" I asked. She said nothing, but opened her arms. We hugged and prayed before she smiled and said Goodbye. It occurred to me that Delissa had a way of ministering to me that was remarkable. Her presence invariably lifted my spirits. In a wondrous quixotic twist of fate she always brought me the joy she sought from me. I always felt better because of her visits.

Reflection has convinced me that this ability to lift the spirit of others is a Heaven-inspired gift. There are those men and women who have the innate ability to make others feel good in their presence. It is truly a God-given gift. Those who possess it have no need to work at making guests feel relaxed. Something in their voice, their mannerisms, their body language, their countenance makes you feel at home and at ease. They are the ones you invariably seek out when a listening ear is needed. And when you leave them you are always the better for having been with them. Those who have one such friend are most fortunate. Those who *are* such persons are blessed indeed.

Like most churchgoers, Delissa occupied the same seat in church each Sabbath. I studied the congregation from my vantage point on the rostrum. I was satisfied to find her routinely in her place. If she was absent, I made it my business to visit her apartment. Characteristically, she could be found with Bible in hand, listening to a tape of one of the services. Her heart and soul were in church even when her body was not.

The summer moved uneventfully. The church was buzzing with summer activities with Delissa taking her vigorous part. Rarely did she miss a service. Her health appeared to be holding up well. She was so buoyant and upbeat and cheerful that one could imagine years of happy, active life awaiting her.

The last time I saw Delissa was a Saturday afternoon after church. For months she had not remained after church to fellowship with those at her eating table, but this afternoon she did. It was like old times. The members of the "cell" were back together at their table in the rear of the hall, eating their fruits and nuts, sharing sandwiches and drinks. She was happy that day; her face was all smiles. How easy it would have been to forget about the insidious interloper that was multiplying itself within her body. The gang was reassembled, and the halcyon days had returned. Perhaps it was the warm, sunny weather. Perhaps it was that special joy that comes from fellowship with brothers and sisters in Christ. We laughed hard that day and celebrated our Christianity. We reveled in the fact that we were one in Christ. It was innocent, simple, plaintive fun, almost childlike in its effect.

In August of that year I was called away for a week. Word reached me that Delissa was taken to the hospital. Being familiar with the course of patients who were HIV positive, I was not too concerned, as this was her first hospitalization. Her husband had already had three or more such hospital stays, which were typical for AIDS patients. I made a mental note to stop in and see Delissa on my first day back. She entered the hospital on Sunday. Word reached me that she died on Wednesday, and, in my absence, her funeral was on Friday. The rapid succession of events was mind-boggling.

A close friend, commenting on Delissa's demeanor during her last days, later told me that she was a marvel. She sang away her hours in the hospital. She refused to watch television but spent most of her waking hours preaching to the doctors and nurses, sharing her faith, and singing. Her friend added, smilingly, that Delissa's singing must have been a chore to listen to because we all knew that singing was not one of Delissa's strengths. When it came to singing, Delissa fell into the "make-a-joyful-noise" category. To her credit, she always sang loudly and lustily and from the heart. But by her own admission, beautiful and melodious it was not. Her firm, resolute faith was much appreciated by the hospital personnel, and even her "singing" was a blessing, I was later told.

Delissa never did get sick, aside from the occasional upset stomach or headache and infrequent, short-lived bouts of general physical fatigue. She was never felled by the numerous opportunistic infections that had befallen so many other AIDS sufferers, including

DELISSA

her husband. She was taken to the hospital on a single occasion and in three days fell peacefully asleep in Jesus. No pain, no struggle. The doctors had no rational explanation for what had happened. Her attending physician, a veteran of the AIDS wars, was beside himself. "It was as though a clock went off in her body. This is most atypical for AIDS patients. She went to sleep and just didn't wake up. I guess it was a heart attack, but not typical. Not typical at all. We will have to call it complications due to AIDS, but this one is strange, real strange," he said.

As I shook his hand, I thought, "Maybe not so strange, not when you know that God takes care of His own." Delissa didn't want to be sick. She asked God for that blessing, and God gave her the desire of her heart. She trusted Him, and He vindicated her trust. The doctors could not explain that which every child of God knows and can affirm even in the face of death—that God is good and merciful.

I took a few minutes to explain Delissa's history to her doctor. I wanted him to understand that the thing that appeared so strange to him had its explanation in the divine will and love of Jesus.

In my years in the ministry I have seen the movings of this Jesus. I have seen Him heal cancer patients. I have watched Him heal a sick teenager in minutes after the family and I had come together for prayer. I had seen my college roommate walk away from a flattened Volkswagen that should have killed him. I have seen Him preserve the life of a boy who had taken two bullets. I have seen believers brought back literally from death's door.

I have come to know and love this Jesus and discern the moving of His gracious hand. I explained to Delissa's doctor that physical healing is not always uppermost in God's mind; salvation is. "Above all else," I told him, "Jesus wants us to be saved, eternally saved. The Lord," I explained, "could have healed her, but she was ready now, so He chose to take her now. That is as much an act of mercy and love as it would have been had you taken a blood test and found her HIV-free. That, the world would say, would be a blessing and a miracle, but I say so is what has happened here."

I noticed that I had his attention and could not resist a sermonette. "Death in Christ is not such a bad thing," I said, fastening my gaze on him. "It is better to die in Jesus than to live without Him. Delissa, dead, might be better off than you and I are alive." His eyes opened wide. I gave him my card as he excused himself and hurried away. I prayed that I had planted a seed.

As mentioned before, my schedule did not allow me to return home to preach the funeral. The family was anxious to have the service quickly. On Friday the church was only partially filled. Word had not filtered to many of the members because of the rapid passing of events. Those attending had many fine remembrances. They listened to a beautiful eulogy of one who, while serving the Lord, was struck down unexplainably. It was a joyous occasion, I was told, if indeed a funeral can be joyous, because all present knew that she died at peace with her Maker.

Delissa was the only one of the three women in this book whose funeral I did not preach. My conversation with the doctor and others took place in the weeks following her death. I was pleased to recall that my last meeting with her was a happy one. I remember her still as the happy, laughing, joyous Christian that exchanged fruit and nuts at the table in the rear of the fellowship hall. I have no doubt that the faith that marked her days sustained her during her last days.

Delissa, of all the people whom I have met, remains one of the greatest women I have ever known. She, in her own way, was a queen—a spiritual paragon; her life, her living, her loving are equal to those of the finest women the world has ever known.

I am not sure where she is buried; the family wished it so. I am sure, however, that there is One who has faithfully marked the spot.

DELISSA

Although she was not great in the eyes of this world, she no doubt is accounted among the greatest in the kingdom of heaven.

How often have we heard it said that love is a high and holy principle? How many times have we read 1 Corinthians 13 and seen listed there all of the God-breathed ingredients that make for true love? How many times have we seen what passes in this world for love fall so far short of that high and lofty example? And yet there is love in this world—holy, pure, determined love.

I have often said that when we love a person, the first thing we give to them is the power to hurt us. Before the candy and flowers and all of those pleasantries that are exchanged between two lovers, the initial gift—the most important, the most fragile—is the heart. When we love someone, we cede to them an enormous amount of power. When you say, "I love you," you are saying, "I give part of me to you. I am entrusting you with, and trusting you to take care of, the most valuable possession I have—my heart." Oftentimes the person who has been given this treasure is less than worthy. And yet, it is still better to love and to accept its attendant risks than to wall up one's heart inside a fort of disinterest and never give of love.

Delissa loved. She loved deeply and patiently. Like her Lord, she loved unto death, and it was that love that sustained her in the murky hours before her passing. It has occurred to me that love can, indeed, get us into trouble, but that same love will see us through that trouble and out of it.

Genesis 1 tells us that in the beginning God created us. This was a creative act of love. Mankind has turned from God, wounded Him, rejected Him. What is God's answer? To reject in turn? To wound as He was wounded? To erase all and start with another Adam? No. God's way out was to employ the same thing that got Him in—love. "For God so loved that He gave," the Scripture says.

Love got Him into the sin predicament, and love was the answer to that predicament. It follows, then, that love, and only love, will see us through. "He that loveth not knoweth not God; for God is love," (1 John 4:8). The Bible then asks us to let this mind (God's mind) be in you. That is to say that we must be like God in our living.

If that is true, then any problem that we ever have can be addressed and redressed and overcome if we will but love enough. If we truly love our God and have allowed Him to live out His love in and through us, we can never truly be cast down or destroyed. We may get hurt or wounded or may even lose our lives, but in loving we will have won. Our God, the Lord, the Originator and the Essence of true love, will see to that.

I would never trivialize anyone's trials, for we each have our crosses to bear, and what might appear to be a light thing to one might be a grievous cross to another—and yet how often we lose heart under the lightest of affliction! How quickly we give up on ourselves and our God in the face of adversity! I have heard it said that if we would truly look at the crosses that many of our fellows are called to bear, we would rejoice and be more thankful for the Lord's mercy toward us.

I once heard a story of a little boy who was riding in his parents' car on the way to church. He had a small part on the Sabbath School program. His line was simple—"trust in God." In his nervousness, he could not remember the three words so he wrote them down on a piece of paper and was rehearsing them in the back seat of the car as the family sped along the highway.

Suddenly, a gust of wind blew through the car, snatching his paper and carrying it out of the window. "Daddy, Daddy," he screamed, "stop the car; my trust in God just flew out of the window!"

When the winds of strife blow through our lives, how many times has our trust in God flown out of the window? How many times do we blame God or accuse God or even curse God, not know-

DELISSA

ing that a loving, caring Savior will give us no more than we can take and support us through it all?

I have asked and others have asked, why would God allow what happened to Delissa? How could He allow something like this to happen to one who obviously loved Him so very much? Perhaps it is precisely because she loved Him so much that God allowed this trial. For only one who knew that depth of love could have carried so heavy a cross with the grace and strength of Delissa. Oddly enough, "Why me?" was the one question Delissa never asked. She never questioned the Lord in that way. I don't know if the thought ever entered her mind. If it did, it was never voiced. She was too fixed, too focused, on heaven. She seemed to know that her situation was not a commentary on her life, her faith, her relationship with Jesus or His love for her.

In the same year of Delissa's passing, I was called to separate two female choir members who had actually begun to wrestle and push one another in the robe room after service. They evidently had become fond of the same gentleman. The two ladies, both attractive, older women with grown children of their own, sought to solve their dilemma through force.

I met with each woman separately and with the brother in contention. Each woman rehearsed a protracted list of supposed atrocities that the other had inflicted upon her and how each felt that if she didn't have this man, this choice prime cut of humanity, she would just die. As I mediated this dispute, I thought of a woman who had a man and did die. One who never raised her voice or her fists, who never lashed out or hit back. I found it somewhat difficult to mediate this indecorous brawl in the light of what Delissa, their sister in Christ, was going through. I longed to tell these two pugilists how sad and inane and ungodly their battle was and that in that same choir was someone fighting an invisible foe that could not be beaten with fists.

I WILL FEAR NO EVIL

Coincidentally, the brother over whom the two were at war had no real love for either, but had relished dating them both. As a handsome, but older man, he enjoyed the attention of not one, but two attractive women, both several years younger than he.

When I was in college, one of the choirs I was in sang a song, one line of which went, "Lord, don't move that mountain; give me strength to climb it. Please don't move that stumbling block—just lead me, Lord, around it." The fact of the matter is that trouble comes in this life, and Christians get their share. To borrow words from Mylon LaFevre's song, "Like rain to a garden when the ground becomes hardened, I know [He's] using it all to help me grow."

A guest on my television show once said that we see God better on the mountain, but we get to know Him in the valley. Delissa obviously knew Him, and her faith held firm even in the valley of the HIV shadow. Praise God, that courage is available to us all.

One of the most difficult words to define is "faith." The simplest definition, perhaps, is "belief." But faith, true biblical faith, is that and much more. It is a belief that moves its possessor to act in concert with that belief. True biblical faith is a God-given bequest that serves as the foundation for, as well as the architecture for, God-ordained action. If you have faith, then that faith animates and informs all that you do. When you are tested, that faith grows and is revealed. Faith is the inevitable consequence of a committed, loving relationship with Jesus.

You should not, can not, work to make your faith stronger. None of us gets to choose our challenges and trials. (Although we do back into many trying situations and bad experiences as a result of the exercise of our own willful, selfish, sinful natures.)

We don't get to select the points at which our faith will be tested. God knows where we need the work. What we need to do is work at walking with, working with, living with and for Jesus. As we open up ourselves to His indwelling and allow Him to take possession of our lives, He will lead us over, under, around, and through life's trials. This journey through life, as orchestrated by the Lord, will simultaneously be an ascent into the cosmos of faith.

From my vantage point, true faith is something that is implanted at the conversion experience and that grows and expands until it fills the life and consumes its host. It envelops and surrounds and colors all that we see and do. Most importantly, it reaches out and back to God, its Author. It fastens its iron grip on the arm of the Savior and, like Jacob of old, refuses to let go until it has received the desired blessing. It stabilizes and secures us. It anchors and holds us fast in the midst of life's severest storms. As it did with Delissa, faith will arm you with the knowledge that with Jesus you can do anything but fail.

Please know, my fellow pilgrim, that in the worst of life's trials you are not alone. You are taken care of. You need not fear. You have a loving, caring Savior. He is greater than the shame, greater than the pain, greater than the rejection of friends, greater even than death.

One of the first texts I committed to memory is Joshua 1:9. The Lord spoke to Joshua at a time in his life when he was about to step into an arena that was unfamiliar and foreboding. The future for Joshua was uncertain and shadowy. Into this haze stepped God, saying, "Have not I commanded thee? Be strong and of a good courage; be not afraid, neither be thou dismayed: for the Lord thy God is with thee whithersoever thou goest." You are not alone. Fear no evil. God is with you.

I Will Fear No Evil

CHAPTER THREE

Tamara

"YOU DO STUFF WHEN YOU'RE HOOKED"

I had noticed her, which was not difficult because she was a strikingly attractive young lady at first glance. People were aware of her presence when she entered a room. A closer look revealed the sad truth that the consequences of a failed marriage and a burgeoning drug addiction were taking their toll on her mentally and physically.

My eyes and mind were forced to draw these conclusions as she sat across the desk from me this bright, cheerful Sabbath morning. I listened to her soft, engaging voice—articulate, direct, intelligent. It belied her background, the history of which I was aware. I knew she was from the south Bronx, grew up in a broken home, was married as a teenager, then separated and divorced not long afterwards. I knew she was mothering two sons, had had an unsuccessful stay in Miami, spent time on welfare and poor paying jobs. I knew she possessed only marginal marketable skills and yet was a fighter. That was the word that best described her—"fighter." She was a pretty, soft-spoken, almost shy woman with a warm heart, living in a fifteen-story, south Bronx apartment building whose elevator, far too often for my taste, did not work.

TAMARA

Rebecca, who was Tamara's mom, possessed computer skills and was constantly in school upgrading them. She possessed a quick, cheery smile that was dampened only by the all-too-frequent asthma attacks that cut her breath and rendered her almost helpless. She was a true fighter who kept an immaculately tidy apartment in a building that ranged from unkempt to outright filthy. She was working class, but she never allowed her financial or social standing to affect her grace or self respect. She radiated a kind of quiet dignity you had to admire. She had raised two children of her own—one a musically talented son who was doing well, and Tamara, the one sitting across from me.

Rebecca was a fighter all right—one who would not be defeated. She raised her kids alone, no help, no charity, no welfare. I remember praying once that her inner fighting spirit would surface as she collapsed in church under the weight of a particularly ferocious attack of asthma. The next Saturday she was back in church, smiling that shy, quiet smile through her labored breathing. Oh yes, Rebecca was a fighter, and she had bequeathed her quiet inner strength to Tamara, whose own asthmatic condition reminded me that inner strength was not all she inherited from her mom.

Tamara's story hurt deeply. They had come so far, this family of fighters, but the battle scars were showing. As a pastor in New York City, after a number of years I had learned to pick up and read signs that perhaps would go unnoticed by a neophyte. Reports had begun to filter through to me that Tamara had been asking various church members for money—small sums, five dollars here and there, occasionally fifteen, but never more than twenty. Of late, the requests had been coming with increasing frequency, accompanied by a request to keep the loan a secret from her mom. This along with other unmistakable signals said one thing—crack addiction. Crack, the latest in a line of demonic derivatives of cocaine, had quickly become the drug of choice in the late '80s, taking its place at the head of the line. It was, and is, far more available than its more expensive cousins, coco paste and powdered cocaine. Resembling a small white pebble and sold in tiny glass or plastic vials, it can be hidden and smoked in a cigar or cigarette or pipe. In New York City crack is everywhere. It has completely changed the face and quality of life in many neighborhoods. It has made law enforcement a game of life and death. Crack cocaine has squeezed itself into places that other forms of cocaine have not gone.

I searched my mind and couldn't remember the days before crack. I had heard the word so much, so often. This wasn't the first time I had confronted this demon that was destroying our children at an unprecedented rate. I had known of babies born addicted to crack through the actions of mothers whose sole concern in life was "getting fixed." I had a goddaughter who was a "crack baby," and I knew of many young people who just wanted to experiment and did not know of crack's insidious ability to seize and hold its prey in an almost unbreakable addictive vice after a single sampling.

Tamara was becoming another of crack's victims. Whether for escapism or as a lark or on a dare, the reason why she took the first smoke did not matter; the fact was that she was now a crack slave. Her internal weapons, which for so long had allowed her to defeat the enemies of her soul, were powerless when arrayed against the new foe.

She was losing battles daily. Spiritually, she was riddled with holes and hemorrhaging badly. My heart ached for her as we sat in my study that Sabbath morning. Although the sun shone brightly through the multi-colored panes of the stained glass windows, a dark gloominess pervaded my office as Tamara poured out her heart to me.

"Does Jesus love me?" she asked. My assurances that He did caused no change in her tired eyes. No response. "But I have made a lot of mistakes," she said, uncrossing her legs and wringing her hands.

"Me, too," I said. "Yeah! I haven't always been a pastor, Tamara, and certainly there were times when I was no angel." Somehow those words seemed to comfort her. Her expression changed, and she sat up with her eyes focused on mine.

I seized the moment. "I am sure that Christ has forgiven me because He has promised me forgiveness."

"But, pastor," she said, "I screwed up big time."

"Christ offers big time forgiveness," I replied. "The Bible says He is able to save to the uttermost. Christ isn't turned off by your failures."

"But you don't know what I've done," her voice began to crack, and tears welled up in the corners of her eyes.

"I don't need to know."

The words seemed to insult her. She sat upright. "You don't want to know?"

"I don't *need* to know, but if you want to talk . . . ."

She cut me off in mid sentence. "Yeah, yeah. I've got to talk . . . to somebody . . . tell you. I, I gotta talk. I messed up so bad; my life, everything. It's all such a mess." The tears were flowing now. "It's all such a big, big mess." Her head dropped, and she became silent. I was not impressed to speak. The next words had to come from her.

"I am on crack," she said with her head still buried in her hands.

"I know," I said. My terse response had its desired effect. Her head popped up, a look of surprise on her small sculptured face. It occurred to me at that moment that a person could read this girl's soul through her eyes. Everything about her appeared in her eyes. Love, hate, surprise, disappointment, sadness, joy, loneliness were all plainly seen in her large, expressive eyes.

She had a pretty face. Dusky brown skin surrounded by a full head of dark brown hair that framed that face, the focal point of which were those eyes. When you looked at her, you were drawn to her eyes—those large, riveting, even sensual windows to her soul. What eyes she had! Expressive, plaintive, innocent.

She tended to do little twitching things with her lips. She often bit them or pursed them, and I mused over the awful beating they must have taken whenever she was very nervous. But, indeed, if nervousness was expressed by the manhandling of her lips, every other emotion was reserved for her eyes. Those large, majestic pools graced by long lashes that blinked furiously when puzzled. They flashed when pleased and drooped at the corners when saddened or pensive and filled with tears when hurt.

It occurred to me that Tamara was an inner city misfit. In a town where poker-faced liars and con men ply their trade with masterful skill, shamming and skimming millions of dollars from unsuspecting "marks," Tamara would stand out in bold relief. She was a pitiful liar. Her heart could be read through her eyes. Sadly, though, in New York there are others who read eyes. In fact, they are experts at it. Eye reading is their stock in trade. They can tell at a glance who is weak and who is strong; who will be susceptible to their game, who to push their wares upon, and who can be ensnared or taken advantage of. They can spot a "mark" or a "chump" or a weak mind. Oh yes, drug dealers are eye readers, too, expert eye readers, and before our discussion would end this day, I would discover that more than one pusher had looked into the eyes that I was now looking into, and had seen something that they could use, abuse, and exploit.

"Yes, you're right," she said. "So what do you think?"

"I think you're an extremely attractive lady and that Jesus is coming soon," I said with a half smile. The nonsequitur response seemed to distract her and brought a short-lived smile to her face. I often do this when counseling, depending on the case. It is an effort to lighten the moment and to get the mind of the counselee away from the depths of the problem and to arrest what I perceived as a steady and counter-productive descent into despair or self-pity.

TAMARA

I needed information if I was to help, and she was breaking up before my eyes. I hoped this light compliment, coupled with a gospel truth, would do the trick. Her eyes twinkled, and her countenance softened if only for a second. She drew a deep breath and pressed on.

"Crack is so horrible; it makes you do things you don't want to," she said softly.

I riveted my gaze on her. She had to know that she had my complete attention. I knew this was difficult for her. I set my face and determined that whatever she said to me would be met with the same stoic expression. I had learned years before that when counseling a distraught person who is pouring out his heart, you show concern regardless of the nature of what he says. You show care, but you never show shock, surprise, dismay, or a condemning spirit. And you don't glance at your watch. There are two ways that clock watching is perceived—both negative. I did not want her to feel that she was imposing on my time or that I was hurrying her along.

By the time most people reach this point they have been so pilloried by life—and perhaps even spent time in self-scourging—that they can little afford to stand additional condemnation by the pastor. And so I locked in. I stared at her and hung on her every word—no clock, no phone, no one else, just Tamara and me. I would not comment. I would not interrupt. I would not condemn. I had no idea of what to expect, but I knew that she wouldn't be here if it were just a toothache she wished to discuss. I prayed silently, "Lord, give me the words. Please, Jesus, whatever she tells me, give me the right response."

"I tried it about a year ago, crack, I mean," she went on. "It was at a party. This guy, he . . . uh, he was nice, and we talked . . . and he . . . well, he offered it. I refused, but eventually, well, you know, I tried it; and then I was like, you know, I was hooked . . . so fast . . . so fast. I was just hooked."

Tamara was like so many young people—born into a Christian home, surrounded all her life by the trappings and accouterments of Christianity, but never really surrendering to it. She knew who Christ was, but He wasn't in control of her life. She had not fully let go of the world. She had not completely turned from Christ, but she was attempting, as do so many, to hold dual citizenship. She wished to be part of the family of God and the kingdom of heaven without severing long-cherished ties with a secular society. She was now coming to the realization, as have countless others, that this is a spiritual impossibility. Anyone who has tried it knows that you cannot carry valid passports in both worlds.

Christ Himself said, "You cannot serve God and man." No one can serve two masters. Many have tried; none have succeeded. Tamara had tried, and the consequences of her failed experiment had brought her to me this day.

As she paused to collect herself, I thought that this is the kind of young person Satan loves to destroy! A beautiful, statuesque, striking, young, black woman is just what he wants. Although not highly educated, she was extremely intelligent and street smart. She was witty and sharp and filled with promise. She was a prime target all right, the kind that Satan likes to ensnare and capture. She was the kind he grinds his heels into and strips of dignity and self-respect.

There are many forces in this world that take a perverse delight in seeing bright, promising youth reduced to human detritus. Far too many voices call young minds to life's garbage heaps. And many young people follow as if inexorably drawn by some demonic, self-destructive Pied Piper. Some, sadly very few, are able to break away and hear another voice.

As we race into this new century, it has become apparent that fewer and fewer are able to break away. We are losing young and old by the thousands, black and white, rich and poor. Churches, for all their efforts and intentions, often seem to be able to do precious

TAMARA

little to stem the tide. It's as though the corporate Christian community has been reduced to a little boy putting one finger in a massive dike riddled with holes. Not only is the child not mastering the situation, but, indeed, an argument can be made that he is in imminent danger of drowning.

I thought about a childhood friend who was found sitting in his own living room dead from his first experiment with drugs. A second friend, a church member, had just recently written an impassioned letter from the state penitentiary. I recalled a recent visit to Buffalo, New York, and seeing a man on the corner, shoeless, filthy, clad in a tattered jacket with no hat on his head, begging for money in fifteen-degree weather. I was startled to recognize him as a famed high school basketball player from my youth. I was a good basketball player, but he was great. I used to wish and pray that I could be like him. Basketball wasn't everything to me; it was to him. When my ball-playing days were over, I became a minister. He became a bum!

Yes, indeed, youth are the ones that Satan loves. He shines the bright light in their eyes. He entices and cajoles them, and when he has them in his clutches, he debases and degrades them. In this age when the bottom is reached so quickly, by the time the victim awakens from his stupor, it is too late. The laughter that is heard is no longer the joyous revelry of well-wishing comrades and admirers. It is the cynical, self-satisfied snicker of the devil who has closed the door and turned the key on their cage, leaving them with the parting malediction: "So long, sucker!"

Tamara was now hearing the faint pleading of that alternate call—that still, small voice of God—and I was determined to amplify that voice so that its message would become loud and clear in her heart and mind.

"He was my contact," she continued. "He got it for me, the crack, and sometimes I would get it on the street if I couldn't find him. But he was my regular. I didn't have enough money, so sometimes he would get me some if I did stuff with him. When you are hooked, you do stuff, you know, with guys. You do stuff, and you're sorry, but you do it because you are hooked and you have to, know what I mean?"

She opened those magnetic eyes and trained them on me—looking, searching for some sign. It occurred to me that she was trying to gauge my response. She peered at me, and we sat searching each other's faces. She would not drop her eyes, and I would not surrender by dropping mine. Furrowing my brow, I softened my gaze in an effort to let her know that it was all right to go on. I was not there to condemn her, just to listen and point her to forgiveness. She drew a deep breath and continued.

"It affects you; it makes you crazy." She re-crossed her legs and resumed her hand wringing. "Sometimes you feel dirty; you think everyone's talking about you and looking at you and stuff. I have two sons . . . I am a mother . . . I have to take care, but you get so messed up." Her last sentence broke up, and the tears came again, followed by sobs which quickly became heavy crying accompanied by a soul-rending moan.

The intensity of her crying somewhat unsettled me. I grabbed some tissue and handed them to her. I walked around my desk and sat next to her. I took her hand and whispered, "It's OK." As if by instinct she rested her head on my shoulder, her tears quickly soaking my jacket, her arm encircling my waist and squeezing me as she sobbed. The red light went on! "This will never do," I thought.

Her hair was brushing my cheek; her perfume filling my nostrils; her body warmth invading my space. She was too young, too attractive, and this was not right. My "uncool situation" meter was in the red zone, and I had to find a way to extricate myself without hurting her feelings. I certainly didn't want her to feel rejected, but she was too cute and too close. I didn't want to upset her, but I

TAMARA

didn't need to have my equilibrium upset either.

It occurred to me that if one of the church's "wagging tongues" were to walk in at that instant, this situation might prove difficult to explain. This was a very real possibility as it was my custom, when counseling certain females under fifty years of age, to leave my office door unlocked. This procedure, I felt, discouraged rumors, and since well over half of my congregation was female, it ameliorated the possible negative impact of the substantial amount of time I had to spend counseling women.

I stroked her hair precisely two times. "It's all right; Jesus knows; Jesus knows," I said softly.

"It's funny," I thought later, "how simply mentioning the name of Jesus changes things." Lives change; situations change; problems change; the mere mention of the name Jesus can diffuse a ticking time bomb or cool down something that is getting a little too hot. Or if needed, the name of Jesus can heat up something that has grown cold. It can also bring you back to center when you are in danger of going off track. Perhaps one or two televangelists who have run into trouble should have used it. It is good counsel for all pastors and counselors.

Things just seem to go better when the name of the Savior is called. The mood in the room changed, and things settled down. Tamara sat up, wiped her tear-stained face, and continued. "I lost one job, but got another. I don't know . . . these jobs . . . it seems like it's worse on the weekends, the crack thing, I mean. Seems like every Friday night, just before Sabbath, it's just on me like a monkey, a gorilla, an elephant on my back, and I can't resist. You know, you can't resist it when it gets like that. I try to pray, but, . . . " She stopped, visibly fighting back tears. "I'm OK; I'm fine," she said, her voice now more controlled. "Last night it was real bad. It's never been like this before. I couldn't sleep or eat. I was sweating and throwing up. The kids were asleep, and Mom was asleep too. I was tossing in bed, wide awake and running to the bathroom every fifteen minutes to puke my guts out. I have some gum that's supposed to stop it, but it wasn't working. You know, sometimes when people are all around, you feel so alone!"

"Yeah, I know," I said softly. I was tempted to break into a story of a time when I felt particularly lonely, a reality that is not uncommon among ministers. Somehow I couldn't get the consent of my mind to do it, and anyway, I thought, she wasn't there to hear any pseudo sob story from me. It would not do her any good at this point. I mentally slapped myself for being so presumptuous, kept my mouth shut, and listened to her.

"I held out as long as I could, and about three o'clock this morning when everyone was asleep, I got up and put on a dress and went out looking for crack that I had no money to buy."

How ironic, I thought. I knew of grown men—big, strong, able men—who would not venture out into the back streets of the Bronx at 3:00 A.M. on a Saturday morning. But to a little woman, weighing not much more than 115 pounds and enslaved by drugs, fear and danger were not a deterrent. The only reality was drugs. The habit had to be satisfied; the appetite had to be satiated. The time of day, the imminent danger, the ever-present prospect of death meant nothing.

I recalled a story that had recently appeared in the papers concerning a ten-year-old boy arrested at 2:00 A.M. with just short of five thousand dollars in his pockets. This ten-year-old was not a buyer, but a dealer. He was also carrying a fully loaded gun. This frightening reality was Tamara's world. Guns, drugs, secret meetings, darkened alleys, loneliness, desperation, enslavement. It saddened me to think that as heaven gazed down that early Saturday morning, it probably viewed hundreds, perhaps thousands, of Tamaras in the Bronx and across New York City. I was sure that Tamara felt alone, but the truth was that she had a lot of silent,

TAMARA

suffering company as she slipped out of the house in the wee hours of that morning.

There are hundreds of thousands of drug addicted persons in New York City. Many, both male and female, prostitute themselves or are reduced to stealing, panhandling, burglary, or selling drugs. I was involved with a mayoral commission on drugs that pegged the number of intravenous drug users in the city at about 475,000. That number did not include sniffers, snorters, and smokers. That was a number identifying known needle users in New York City. It didn't begin to cover the thousands of unknown users and those who, like Tamara, smoked their dope rather than injected it.

Drug abuse makes one desperate, and desperate people do desperate things. Tamara spoke, bringing me back from my thoughts. "It didn't take long. I spotted someone whose face I had seen around. His body language suggested that he was selling; mine suggested that I was buying. Just like that, no words, done deal. On the street there's not a lot of conversation. Nobody's out to get acquainted and certainly not to make friends. You don't want to know them, and they don't want to know you. It's not social. You do what you have to do and disappear. Most of the people on stuff hate their suppliers," she said meditatively. "They hate the drugs, and they hate themselves. Can a person really hate himself?"

I asked her if she hated herself, and she responded, "I hate what I am."

"What are you?" I asked.

"The kind of person you wouldn't talk to if you really knew me."

"Maybe you wouldn't talk to me if you really knew me," I said. "Let's just say we are two lost souls looking for some light."

"Yeah, but something tells me I'm a little more lost."

"Hey, lost is lost," I said.

Tamara sighed and continued her narrative. "He walked along

the street and turned into an alley. I followed. He saw me shaking and knew that I needed it bad. He tried to jack up the price from five dollars to ten. I asked him to give me a break, and he went back to five. He took two crack vials from his pocket and quickly squeezed them into my hand. 'Come on, come on, the bank (money),' he sort of growled at me.

"I told him I don't have any money, but I could get some tomorrow if he would just let me slide tonight. 'You know me; you know where I live,' I told him.

"He told me that he didn't play that way; it was strictly C.O.D.; no pay, no play. I told him that I had no money. I begged him. Pastor, I was crying and literally begging the man for drugs. I told him that I had nothing to give him, but I needed it. He turned to leave, but stopped. 'Yes, you do have something to give me,' he said.

"He walked over to me. The tone of his voice told me what he wanted. As he walked, I could see it on his face; he wasn't looking at me. He was looking through me like a starving rat at a piece of cheese. His eyes ran up and down me, and I felt naked. In my rush to get out of the house I really hadn't dressed properly. I threw on a dress and not much else. I should have put on a suit of armor," she said with a half smile.

My mind drifted off for a moment, musing over the fact that so many churchgoers are willing to reveal the most intimate aspects of their personal lives to their pastor and what a tremendous burden that places on the clergyman. I recalled the time during a hospital visit a female member had lifted her hospital sheet to show me a burn she had suffered on the upper section of her inner thigh. Or the expectant mother who placed my hand under her blouse so I could feel the kicking of her soon-to-be-born child. I thought about a fellow pastor who, fortunately with his wife, visited a member who in a fit of unabashed euphoria lifted her blouse to proudly

TAMARA

display the results of a recent breast-reduction surgery.

Over the years I had been exposed to the intimacies of lives lived by people who were less than perfect. Most of the details were unsolicited, and yet early on I discovered the cathartic value of allowing a counselee to totally unburden himself. Usually, when he or she begins to speak and the dam bursts, there is no way to alter or abate the flow. Whatever self-revealing details wash out have to be taken in stride. If the details are intimate, well that is just a necessary part of flood control and reconstruction.

Tamara, visibly shook as if chilled by a sudden cold wind. "I should have run. My mind said Go, but my legs wouldn't move. I just stood there and let him come closer. I could smell the liquor on his breath as he reached around and put his hand on my rear. He squeezed and rubbed me and laughed."

Her eyes were wide now, no tears, and although the memories were vivid and painful, she appeared determined to press on. She seemed angry more than hurt; an anger laced with sorrow, but she felt she needed to tell me, and I felt I needed to listen.

As she spoke, my mind conjured up images of this beautiful young girl being pawed and fondled by a sleazy somebody who sold death for a living. I was angry, and I wanted to cry for her, for me, for the thousands who daily carry their pain like so much excess baggage that they cannot shed. Baggage that slows their pace so that they can no longer keep up with society. Each day finds them falling further and further behind until they are so far away that we can no longer see them or their hurt; and once out of sight, they are soon forgotten. I couldn't help those thousands, but I could help this one. I was determined to see it through.

"He squeezed me," she continued, "pulling me to him, saying 'Yeah, baby, you got plenty to give.' I should have screamed or said No or fought or just said 'Forget it!' Drug dealers don't like noise, and he would have split. But I didn't." She stopped cold, her eyes staring at me, but not seeing. She was reliving the incident in her mind. Her face contorted, and her lips pursed. Her left hand, which had for so long gripped her chair, flexed and balled itself into a tight fist. She pounded lightly on her thigh as she continued.

"I let him touch me and handle me, and I said nothing; I did nothing. I just let it happen 'cause I'm addicted, and when you're, you know, addicted, you just do stuff. He put his hand under my dress, and then I was on the ground with my dress up. The smell of wine and dog feces, garbage and urine, and some strange man pushing himself into me. He didn't care about me. He didn't even look at my face the whole time he did it. Maybe if he had he would have seen how much I hated what he was doing. Maybe he would have seen my tears. He was hurting me, and I was crying, but he just kept on till he was finished. He got off me and gave me the crack. He made some remark about driving a hard bargain, laughed, and walked away. I got up, pulled down my dress, and did the crack right there in the alley. Then I went home and took a long shower, but still felt dirty. I feel so unclean sometimes. I thought about my life. It's Friday night. I'm going to church tomorrow. It's 3:00 o'clock in the morning, and I am on the ground. A man is on me and in me, and I don't even know his name. All this for drugs."

Tears cascaded down her cheeks, but she refused to acknowledge or accept them. As though fighting a battle with her own emotions, the mind appeared to be in combat with the heart. She accepted the tissue I gave, but would not dry her reddened eyes. One would not even know that she was crying. There were no moans, no sounds, no halting speech. She sat steady and strong, except for the torrent of tears exiting those sad expressive eyes.

"Did you ever stop to think about all the diseases that are sexually transmitted? In this world you can pay a stiff penalty for sex. You can pick up something and one day wake up dead," I told her. "There is a lot of stuff out there. Two or three vials of crack aren't worth your life, are they?" Her eyes answered the question.

"That sounds rational now, but last night I wasn't thinking rationally," she said, shrugging her shoulders.

I paused for a moment, taking in the depth of the story I had just heard. My heart was pounding like a trip hammer. If I were white, my face would have been beet red. The constellation of emotions flashing through my mind was difficult to process. I was attempting to maintain a semblance of cool, but this story was bowling me over. It was up around my throat, and the pity and sorrow and anger for what Satan was doing to this beautiful child was engulfing me. I needed a second or two to regroup. It was quite a saga, and I wanted my response to be correct. "You have used the words 'addict' and 'addicted' a lot today. Do you think that you are addicted?" I asked.

"Today is the first time that I've said that, but yeah, I must be. A person wouldn't do some of the things that I have been doing the last few weeks unless they were addicted."

"Admitting that is a step in the right direction. It's hard to get found unless you admit that you are lost. What do you want?" I asked quietly, again training my eyes squarely on her.

"To be normal, to be happy, to be free like I used to be," she answered, her voice trailing off as if she were mentally retreating to a happier time and place.

"How badly do you want that?"

The question seemed to throw her. "I don't understand. What do you mean?" her eyes asked the question before it came from her mouth.

I said: "I have counseled a lot of people who want their lives to be straight and neat and tidy, but they aren't willing to make any sacrifices and lifestyle changes to secure that neatness. They want the pastor or better, God, to wave a magic wand and wipe away the consequences of decisions they have made or situations that they have gotten themselves into. Occasionally, the Lord does; most often He does not, and for good reason.

"If we could snap our fingers and change circumstances, we would have less motivation to live right because if we did wrong, we could wish and pray it away in an instant. Our walk into sin is a slow step-by-step journey, and so our walk to freedom must also be a step-by-step journey. Usually the walk out is much more painful than the walk in, but that pain serves as conditioning should we ever be tempted to reverse our course and move back into sin. It is those victories, hardest fought and won, that are most precious to us.

"If gold were easy to get, everyone would have it. I need to know if you are prepared for a fight. Jesus is, but He can't do it without you. As powerful as God is, He can't salvage you if you are determined not to be saved. He won't bring you kicking and screaming into salvation. He's going to need your cooperation and your commitment. If you give Him those, together there is nothing you can't do. He's ready. He's willing. He's able. And He's waiting for you to push the start button."

For the first time in thirty-five minutes her eyes left mine. She stared pensively at the colored panes of the stained glass windows, her finger running along the lead tracery that secured each pane. "Um . . . huh . . . yes, I'm ready; as ready as I'll ever be." The words came in a long, low sigh. "If I don't change, I'll die."

"Tell me, Tamara, Who is Jesus?"

The eyes again expressed puzzlement, but she responded: "He's God; the Son of God. He made everything. He's Lord of the Sabbath. He's our Mediator."

I smiled to myself. She was parroting the things she had learned in church school and from sermons, the things she thought I wanted to hear. I was content to follow this course for a while. Soon I interrupted, "That's all good, Tamara, but what does He mean to you? Who is Jesus to you? Who is He to you?"

TAMARA

"I don't know," she said, squirming for the first time since coming into my office. "He must hate me. I guess He's disappointed in me, especially when I keep making the same mistakes and doing the same things. He must get so tired. I don't pray much. I come to church, but sometimes my mind is some place else. I guess I'm not the best church member in the world."

"Does Jesus love you?" I asked. She froze, her face blank, her eyes open and staring into mine, her lips parted slightly as if to speak, but no response. She had no answer. I pressed on. "Do you love Him?" Her head dipped slightly as if to speak, but no reply.

I thought I would ask her a question that she could answer, even if the answer was only "I don't know." "Which of the two do you think is more important—you loving Him or Him loving you? This line of questioning was unnerving her. I don't believe that she had ever given it any real thought. She had been driven by events and had accepted the notion that Christ took no notice of, or had no time for, people like her. Like others, she attended church as a matter of routine, looking for, but not allowing herself to find, peace in Jesus. She had no real idea of what Jesus thought of her. She assumed that He must feel about her the same as she often felt about herself—ashamed, fed up, and disgusted. And yet, beneath it all there was an unexpressed hope—a hope that she could not articulate. Even now, when asked to give voice to that hope, her fear and uncertainty stayed her tongue and froze her in her seat.

"I think it's important for you to know and believe that Jesus loves you. Your mistakes don't turn Him off," I repeated. "He is not repulsed by you. He is not waiting with a mouth full of 'I told you so's.' All He has is love and concern and forgiveness in store, but you can't get into the storehouse without a key, and He has, no, He *is* that key. It doesn't matter so much how you feel; just now, the most important thing is that He loved you first. He's been ready for you for a long time, and now you are ready for Him. Believe me,

I WILL FEAR NO EVIL

He has the answer to your questions. The Bible says we love Him because He first loved us. Christ has the ability, Tamara, to separate the act from the person—something we humans have trouble doing. He hates sin, but loves the sinner. Even when you were in the alley last night, Jesus loved you. It wasn't hate or disgust that He felt; it was love, compassion, pity, and concern. He saw you when no one else did, and He was in every tear. He had the power to keep you in the house last night if you had allowed Him, and He has the power to keep you from now on."

I stopped to catch my breath. I could scarcely believe myself. I was droning on like a runaway freight train. I so desperately wanted her to know and feel Christ's love, and time was now against us. She had to understand that Jesus was not her accuser, but her Defender and Deliverer. I began to notice a response to my sermonette. Her eyes softened. I saw signs of relief. Until now, I was not sure if anything that I was saying was getting through, but those words seemed to help.

We talked about King David—murderer, wife stealer, and adulterer. The one of whom God said, "He is a man after My own heart."

"If God can say that of David after his transgressions, He can say that of you," I told Tamara. The key, I said, was that David, when caught, didn't seek to cover his sins or excuse them. He readily admitted his sinful course and threw himself on the mercy of God. I quoted David: "Lord, whatever is necessary to get my soul right with You, I'll do." Then I asked her, "Are you willing to make that statement?" She nodded, and I continued. "If we confess our sins, He is faithful and just to forgive . . . and cleanse from all unrighteousness. How does that sound to you?" I asked with a big smile.

Tamara said softly, "Sounds good."

I replied, "Good, I just made it up." Her eyes responded, and I added, "Oh, come now, Jesus said that, and He had you in mind when He said it." This light banter seemed to lift her spirits. I felt that she needed it. She was keenly aware of the enormity of her sin. I was in no way trivializing it, but she needed a break. I thought of Christ's words to the woman caught in adultery, "Neither do I condemn thee."

Christ was not trivializing that woman's sin, but opted for conciliation over condemnation at that instance, the same option of which I was now availing myself. There were enough people bombarding Tamara with the wrath and justice of God. I thought it good to remind her that God is love. John, in his Gospel, could have said that God is righteousness, sinless, justice, or a million other words, but he chose love. "He that loveth not knoweth not God; for God is love" (1 John 4:8).

"That describes His feelings toward you, and it should describe our feelings," I said to her. "We all must love you as He loves. There is a text we all need to remember—'All have sinned.' Our addiction may not be crack, but we all have something. We all need forgiveness. It's just a request away. Christ can say to you as He did to that woman, 'Go and sin no more.'" I wanted Tamara to know that she was the victim, not the criminal. "If you've got enough sense to call, He's got enough love to answer," I added.

She let out a little squeal and smiled broadly. "Let's pray," I said. We joined hands and fell to our knees. She prayed first. I followed. She asked for forgiveness and pledged to give up crack, with God's help.

I had heard an addict's pledge before. There are those who will tell you that an addict's pledge is like a rope of sand. Personal experience had brought me to reluctant agreement. An addicted person will promise anything; He will say anything. Somehow, though, I believed Tamara. She had nothing to gain by making that promise. She wasn't requesting money, and she certainly wasn't trying to impress me. No, I thought, this decision was coming from the heart. Even if she should later fall and slip back into addiction, this day, at this hour, she was being as truthful as she knew how to be. I felt her sincerity, and as we stood and embraced, I saw in her a peace that I recognized.

So often just sharing the burden lightens the load. I was her accomplice now, a partner sworn to secrecy, an oath that was not given without condition. The secret, such as it was, would be kept if, and only if, she sought professional help. Telling me was just a first step, I counseled her.

As a pastor, I could pray, give spiritual insight, and point the way, but Tamara had to do the walking one difficult step at a time. My promise was good as long as she kept moving forward. "I'm your friend," I assured her. "Jesus is your Friend, also. The three of us, Jesus, you, and me, we'll get you straight. When you get it all together, there will be no more need for secrets." Tamara sighed a long, measured "Yes," as if the mere thought of living drug free lifted a tremendous weight from her slender, overburdened shoulders.

She promised to stop borrowing money from church members and even offered to repay them. I assured her that the latter was not necessary for now and that the church would be better served and more pleased to see her well and happy and free of drugs. Her eyes fairly danced, and she smiled the smile of a woman who had just been given the promise of a future. We stood, embraced, and Tamara made her way out of my office and into the sanctuary. I decided not to attend my Sabbath School class. It was late and I probably wouldn't have heard the teacher anyway. I had precious little time to collect my thoughts before preaching the morning's sermon.

Tamara did make changes, not quick changes, not dramatic ones, but slow, steady changes. The wagging tongues still spoke, but carried a different message. Someone once said that bad news travels seven times around the world before good news gets its pants on. Fortunately, there are times when good news makes the rounds

TAMARA

also, and the obvious change in Tamara became the center of much discussion. Tamara got help for her addition.

Tamara had little time for self-pity. She was in active rehabilitation, working, taking care of two active sons, and living the life of freedom. Her head was free; her heart was free; her system was chemical-free; and this new-found liberty was, itself, intoxicating. She was in a constant state of spiritual inebriation, an infectious drunkenness that made her a delight to be around. She enrolled in a program and took the challenge seriously. She was able to work on an outpatient basis, and we saw each other regularly. Her life seemed settled and ordered. Her skin cleared and brightened, and she walked with an extra bounce in her step.

It amused me to see the reactions of the young men (and of old men, for that matter) when she entered or left a room. She was a head-turner. In fact, she was so attractive that she scared off many potential suitors. Since college days, I have been amazed to see how some of the most beautiful women have been the most lonely. The fragile male ego (mine included), so afraid of rejection, often avoids the most beautiful women. Attractive, even stunning, women sat alone in the dorm or were forced to socialize with their girlfriends on Saturday nights because guys with rejection phobias were too afraid to ask them out.

Luckily, as I grew older and entered the ministry, I totally lost all semblance of that fear. Hey! All they could say was, "No." Who could turn down a safe date with a moderately handsome man of the cloth? Besides, in my church, as in most, there is a disproportionate surplus of females. The intelligent, enterprising young male has his pick. He can be a veritable church mouse in a cheese factory.

It is quite odd how men looking for "girls like the girl that married dear old dad," search the singles bars and night clubs, when the absolute cream of the crop can be found in church. Each week I look into the faces of a sea of attractive, intelligent young ladies, suffering from acute guy shortage. I wish there were a pill that could be slipped into the drinks of men to convert them and make them come to church. Perhaps, we should put a sign over the door reading, "Attractive, intelligent, eligible, Christian young ladies. Inquire within. Only men with honorable intentions need apply."

Tamara got and held a good job, and each week we spoke either in person or on the phone. We developed secret signs and communications. When we met in church, words were unnecessary; I knew at a glance how her week had gone. It was kind of fun to talk to her without words and to look down from the pulpit and carry on a conversation while singing the hymn of the morning.

Tamara had some setbacks. Although she experienced no more frantic 3:00 A.M. searching, her life was not all success and glory. She missed some church and had her down days. Her former friends and suppliers, knowing her weakness, tried desperately to pull her back to the old lifestyle. Even a so-called Christian propositioned her. We discussed these things, and she worked her way through them. Tamara had changed direction, and although she occasionally fell on her journey, I had no doubt that she was moving closer to her Lord and to total recovery. Her children, bright, frisky, aggressive, were in church each week, neatly dressed and orderly. They were joyous, as she was. Each Saturday I looked for them and was disturbed when I did not see them.

I would so have loved to have seen Tamara's complete recovery. To see her come all the way back and to see what she would have done with all the potential she had. But she was never to fill that potential. Four months later, on one of New York's oppressively hot and humid August days, the kind of day that even a person with two healthy lungs and no asthmatic condition finds taxing, her lungs shut down on her. The combination of sun, heat, dirty air, and frail constitution conspired against her overtaxed lungs. She collapsed on the street while traveling home from work. She

TAMARA

was rushed to the hospital but died a few hours later. While she was lying semi-conscious on the sidewalk, the city showed its ugly side as someone grabbed her purse. Since she was unable to speak or identify herself, it was some time before her family was notified.

When I arrived at the hospital, her mother informed me that the game little fighter had lost this final battle with life. She spent her last hours fighting to hold on. Perhaps it was emblematic since she had spent her life fighting against the odds, beating back those forces that would destroy her. In the end, I was later told, she surrendered peacefully. She suddenly breathed her last breath, ended the struggle, and fell asleep in Jesus.

Yes, I thought to myself as we stood on the sidewalk outside the hospital, beneath the same merciless sun that had attacked Tamara, she might have lost this struggle, but she had won the bigger battle. She had faced the dragon, taken his worst, and with Christ's help, defeated him. She had been to hell and back. She had been as low as she had ever dreamed she could be, but she picked herself up and walked out of hell and into the arms of Jesus. Dead or alive, she was safe there.

I preached Tamara's eulogy with joy and peace. I commended her courage and strength to the congregation. I spoke of Mary, who was forgiven by Christ for her transgressions. I assured all present that the same forgiveness was offered to and accepted by Tamara.

Whenever I see two boxers in the ring, I know that one will win and one will lose. I cannot help but think of Tamara, the game little fighter. There is one compelling difference, though. Tamara won. She won big! The fight didn't last long, and she was knocked out early. But she won! She won the grand prize because somewhere between rounds she got Jesus in her corner. She got tired of taking punches and decided to get some protection and strength to fight back.

Tamara died a winner. Her prize? It would take all eternity to describe it.

I WILL FEAR NO EVIL

As I look at today's youth and how different they are from the youth of my time, I am stunned and saddened by the contrast. I imagine that many people have felt that way before. I recall one nineteenth-century writer lamenting the indolence, apathy, and worldliness of the youth of that day. But if, indeed, these things were true more than one hundred years ago, they are even more than true today.

Our youth experience a hopelessness, a helplessness, today that I believe has never existed before. Much of it has to do with television. Though this sounds like a digression, it is not. Although to my knowledge, no formal studies have been done as to the leavening effect of television on the population in general and youth in particular, my one-man anecdotal evidence, gleaned from twenty plus years in urban ministry, says that most of that influence has been negative.

We have and are raising a generation of cynical, self-centered, adrenaline- addicted, media-fed, media-bred youth who are lost and don't know it. And if they are aware of it, they don't care. These are the most dangerous days for youth in the history of the world. We are losing children at every turn. One and a half million babies a year never get the chance to be born; some, due to partial birth abortions, are murdered on their way into life. Statistically, the most dangerous place to be is in the womb of someone who doesn't believe in Jesus. Once a child gets into this world, a staggering array of forces conspire to warp, misshape, and destroy that life if possible.

Sadly, in many cases parents have abandoned their God-given responsibility to train, nurture, direct, and correct their children. And even when parents put forth the effort, society wages a persistent battle to annul the positive effects of that tutelage.

Sex is used to sell everything. We live in a post-Christian age in which the church is no longer the arbiter of morality for society. Politicians speak about moral values when they want our votes, but we are made increasingly aware that their lives are less than exemplary.

Children admit that they don't listen to their parents. Parents admit that they don't talk to their kids. If the truth be known, the most listened-to arbiter in the late 1980s and '90s is the television talk show. The world, old and young, has turned to the talk show for values. These shows are not hosted by individuals chosen for their integrity. This is not to say that talk show hosts as a group are amoral, but it does suggest that when a talk show host is selected, high moral standards fall into line behind looks, charisma, affability, or the ability to be confrontational. The blind are literally leading the blind. Talk shows, like all of television, are driven by ratings rather than by any overwhelming need to set some ultimate moral tone.

The reason so many children are lost is because so many adults are lost. This "lostness" shows itself more in the younger generation and is exacerbated by the inescapable fact that there is simply more danger about today than ever before. There are more ways to be injured, more ways to die. As Tamara's case shows, the consequences for transgression are more severe. If the talk shows have taught us anything, they have made us aware of the pitiful lack of respect for human life that characterizes life in our towns and cities. Gangs have replaced the family, and life is lost at an alarming rate.

In an effort to maintain our own sanity, we have hardened ourselves and closed our ears to the constant barrage of news reports detailing rapes, murders, thefts, purse snatchings, muggings, spousal and child abuse, molestations, knifings, shootings, and such, some committed by surprisingly young people. The *New York Post*, some years ago, carried on its front page the story of a nine-year-old who shot his mother to death because, as he said, she "nagged him for not going to school." The average age at which young girls in New York City begin sexual activity has descended year by year. It is difficult to find a girl in junior high who has not at least experimented with sex. Many are active sexually.

I counseled a young woman in her twenties who unabashedly told me that she had had a number of abortions and was sexually active. When I asked her about the ever-present danger of sexually transmitted diseases, including HIV, her rejoinder to me was that she practiced safe sex, which to her meant that she slept only with married men. She was sad and knew that she was sinning, but she told me, "I've done this for so long, I don't know if I can stop."

I would like you to let that sink in. Don't just be repulsed! Don't just be sad! Don't simply walk by and shake your head. Be hurt! Be moved! For as hard and base as that may sound, it is a fact of life in urban America. People come into and pass out of our churches and lives with troubles that we would never believe. They need help, healing, wholeness! They need Jesus. Can you believe that the person next to you in the pew would live the life this young woman was living? If you knew her life, would you move away? Would you choose another pew? Would you still greet her with a sanctified kiss? Would you pray for and with her?

Would you like some good news now? I have some! She stopped! Yeah!

Jesus did it again! He changed her. Caught her, stopped her, convicted her, converted her. I baptized her, and God added her to His family. She is happy, healthy, alive, and well, and living a life of joy in Jesus.

Impossible, you say! Are you kidding? Nothing is impossible with the Lord. He is able to save to the uttermost, the Bible says. We need to tell that and live that before our young people. We need to show them, more than tell them, that Jesus is a forgiving Lord. If there is one statement that bears repeating, it is that Christ forgives! It simply does not matter what you've done. 1 John 1:9 is emphatic, "If we confess our sins, he is faithful and just to forgive us our sins, and to cleanse us from all unrighteousness." That promise is given

TAMARA

without qualification. As rough, as tough, as ruthless, as relentless as the city is, Jesus is able.

The God of Abraham, Isaac, and Jacob is waiting and longing to be your God. Truly, what He did for them, for Tamara, for others, He can and will do for you. No promise is safer or surer.

Over and over, the Bible, particularly the New Testament, preaches Christ's infinite desire to free us from sin—and from its consequences as far as possible in this life.

Jesus can make us free! What an incredibly sublime thought. The sins that plague you can be vanquished through prayer, through struggle, through the uniting of the will with the omnipotent, indefatigable, unbeatable power of God.

I received a call not long ago from someone who would not give his name. He has a problem. He does not believe he can conquer it. He hates it, and it affects his every waking moment. Having resigned himself to living with it for the rest of his life, he dejectedly said to me after a three-hour conversation, "It's not fair."

Let me say this. In this life, little is fair. We do not get to pick our trials. We must abandon this idea and cry. You will never get healed if you are stuck in the "it's not fair" rut. Of course it's not fair. But it wasn't fair for Jesus to have to die. He never sinned or hurt anyone. He was murdered by those He came to save. No one could help Him; there *is* Someone to help you. Was it fair for us to do that to Jesus? The operative question for healing is not, Why am I here? It is a given that I am here. The question is: Where do I go from here? How do Jesus and I get me from where I am to where He wants me to be?

Be prepared for victory!

I Will Fear No Evil

CHAPTER FOUR

Juliet

"NOBODY KNOWS BUT JESUS"

Even now, as I think of Juliet, pleasant memories come to mind. She was small, just under five feet tall and slightly built. There wasn't much to distinguish her. She didn't stand out in a crowd. She was not outspoken. If one were forced to describe her, I imagine he would employ the word "plain" somewhere in his description. Juliet was not unattractive, but she was not particularly attractive, either. Her clothes were always neat and clean, but not of the nature that would make one take a second look. To see the abundant beauty that Juliet possessed, one had to look beneath the surface.

To some Juliet looked like a child. She certainly was child-sized, and she approached and attacked life with all of the enthusiasm of an adolescent. Her youthful appearance and bubbly countenance belied her years. If she did not have three daughters, one of whom would be married several months after her death, it would have been difficult for her to prove her age. She loved the young, and they, in turn, loved and trusted her. She was at home with them. They often came to her with secrets exposed to no other adults. They were not concerned with her looks or clothes. They saw only

JULIET

a buoyant, caring little pixie who gave of her time, her copious energy, and her love.

Juliet was the classic busy beaver, involved with youth, singing in the choir, and being a compulsive volunteer. Anytime the call went forth for volunteers to man the battlements for whatever program, Juliet's hand was among the first raised. The consummate behind-the-scenes worker, Juliet never asked for the spotlight—indeed, she shunned it. If ever you wanted to see someone squirm, blush, and become downright disquieted, just watch Juliet when forced to suffer through a compliment. I think she actually found them painful, and yet few people deserved them more. She struggled with both private and public praise. If you were to take her aside and thank her for a job well done, she would not look you in the face or respond above a whisper. She would endure your kind words and humbly cut you off if they continued for too long. The entire speech would be delivered to the top of her bowed head; her eyes, riveted to the floor, would not rise until you were quite finished.

As difficult as it was for her to accept a compliment in private, a public compliment was seen as the ultimate affront. She simply didn't handle praise well. When her name was called, she experienced symptoms that reminded one of the flu. Her eyes watered, her nose ran, her blood pressure rose, and her knees shook. If you could get her to a microphone, the only words you could expect in response would be "Thank you!"

She was the kind of person one could easily overlook, a reality that never seemed to bother her. The Lord saw fit, though, to bless her with an infectious, engaging smile, the kind of ear-to-ear, toothy grin that forced you to respond in kind. On a number of occasions, lists of names were read out and kudos were extended to those who had worked to make some church program a success. Invariably, Juliet's name was not mentioned. Her quiet smile said to those around her that the omission was quite all right. One was awed, when in the presence of that smile, to notice how such a small, thin face could support the deepest dimples, flanked by the largest "chipmunk cheeks" you ever saw.

I vividly recall the last time Juliet attended church services. It was a Communion Sabbath. Her naturally small frame had been reduced to skin and bones. During the testimony period after the service, she electrified the church with a personal recitation affirming her faith, trust, and belief in the Lord. She found the strength to flash her trademark smile, and the effort was responded to positively by every person present. The audience was visibly moved, and as I embraced her and felt her head resting on my shoulder, I forgot that she was dying of AIDS. In fact, she was just several weeks from the end. No one knew or suspected how late it was for her. Had we known, it would not have mattered just then, for on that day she was classic Juliet—bright, outwardly happy, that full-face grin flashing for everyone she met.

Her failing strength did not permit her to stand for long, and most of her greeting was done from a seated position. It didn't seem to matter, though. Our little girl, a church favorite, was with us. She was back home among those who loved and respected her quiet courage. Our joy overflowed.

This was the final Communion for the year, a candlelight service that highlighted the year's passing and praised the Lord for His goodness. It was right and fitting that Juliet be there. Somehow it was all that it should be—this tiny woman fighting back with an inner strength. On that day she commanded our respect, and we gave her our love—every ounce of it.

Everyone knew Juliet's case; it was no secret, and she did not try to make it one. It was not something that was discussed over dinner or whispered about in the corners. The news, once it leaked out, shot around the church like wild fire; bad news always does. But after an initial surge, it was not repeated, rehashed, or mused

JULIET

over, because this was Juliet, the beloved little spiritual workaholic who owned our souls. It was our love and respect for her that kept anyone from repeating, let alone embellishing, the tragic story that we all knew.

Her husband, the disease donor, had also once been a church member. Her mother, a loyal, hardworking Christian, holding positions of responsibility and respect in the church, was also much loved. But if life in New York City has taught us anything, it is that the Christian is not immune to disease. AIDS is no respecter of persons, religions, families, or races. It arises in the so-called best and worst of families. It treats all of its hosts the same.

The problem in Juliet's husband's case was drugs—in particular, drugs that are taken through a needle, too often an unclean needle; a shared, unclean needle; a shared, infected, unclean needle.

I do not imagine he knew what he was carrying when he returned to his wife after a short separation. Juliet had no idea of what he was bringing. She was being a good wife. She was taking her estranged husband back, giving him another chance, fulfilling vows that she had made to herself and to her God. He wanted to straighten out a twisted, convoluted life and return to the woman who had given him three children, but it was not to be. His past quickly overtook him, and in the course of time, too quick to mention, he was dead. His passing was all too sad and traumatic.

Their reconciliation was a stormy, short-lived, and aborted one. They were two different people—he with leanings to a New Age faith, and Juliet firmly rooted in her Adventist Christianity. The match was not a good one. Quietly, resolutely, she resisted all his attempts to proselytize her. She wanted no part of his religion. For his part, he had forsaken his Christian roots and found her faith and fidelity a constant irritant. Their experiment at reunification amounted to a few weeks together, accentuated by a number of passionate physical encounters and precious little meaningful conversation. When they tried to talk, they argued, so they avoided talking. For a time the titillation of long-missed sex masked their differences. Conversation centered on the trite and the noncontroversial. True feelings were not expressed. Each kept his innermost emotions discreetly hidden.

Both parties began to realize that the problems were deep and the gulf between their respective philosophies of life irreconcilably wide. Their bodies were frequently together, their minds seldom. In the course of time, their passion waned, and there was nothing to bond or bind them. They were forced to the realization that sex can and does make a good marriage great, but it cannot make a bad relationship good. Uniting bodies augments and enhances a marriage relationship, but it is no substitute for the uniting of minds. It is an easy thing to unite two bodies. Anatomically, this is possible between any two physically normal human beings. The more difficult thing is the uniting of the minds. Sex is in the mind. What is forgotten many times while couples are in the sweaty heat of passion is the fact that if no mental links are forged, the passion will die.

Sex, though expressed through the body, begins in the mind and is a mental exercise as much as a physical one. The sexual act is at the basic "A level" of communication. If two parties fail to communicate at other levels, the communication at the sexual level loses significance and becomes, not communication and affirmation, but the mere scratching of a biological itch.

Juliet's husband, never one to endure an uncomfortable situation for too long, withdrew. He packed and moved out again. Shortly thereafter, it was realized that his death legacy had been passed to Juliet. Her response to this devastating news was to work harder than ever for her God and her church. Her already-delicate constitution fought valiantly against its HIV invader. She pushed her condition from her mind and threw her energies into her work. Perhaps, more than anyone I have ever met, the praise of God was continually on her lips. She was a constant joy to those who, armed with a knowledge of her condition, listened to her testimonies in church meetings. Invariably, they were pregnant with thanksgiving to God. Not once did this little warrior ever give voice to doubt, despair, or self-pity. I do not know what thoughts she entertained in her private moments, but in those times when she appeared in public, she radiated a peace that soared on the wings of the contagious smile that was her quintessential trademark for all of us who knew her.

Though physically the smallest of the three women discussed in this book, Juliet could match hearts with anyone. What she lacked in stature was amply compensated for in character. What God did not give her in body, He more than made up in soul. She attended choir rehearsal and moved boxes and passed out literature and witnessed for the Lord with an apostolic passion that was staggering. She managed to summon the strength to keep up with the youth she so loved. Every time the doors of the church were opened, Juliet was present. Indeed, on a number of occasions the deacon assigned to unlock the doors found her waiting when he arrived.

Juliet's was no last-minute conversion. This was no last-ditch flurry of Christian activity in an attempt to atone for a life of misdeeds. Quite the contrary, this was Juliet the way she had always been—the first to arrive, the last to leave, and the hardest worker while there. Sadly, even an iron will and a faith the size of Mount Everest could not stop the stealthy advance of AIDS. In time, her strength gave way, and her pace slowed. Her life was frequently interrupted by short stays in the hospital.

I recall one Friday morning when my sermon preparation was interrupted by a call from Juliet's mother stating that she had again been rushed to the hospital. I dressed and sped to the emergency room. After having talked my way out of a speeding ticket, I walked in to face the downcast countenances of her mother and oldest child. They had been there for some time and were visibly shaken. This was not Juliet's first bout with pneumonia, and she was not doing well. She had been failing for a few days, and her reluctance to go to the hospital was overridden by her family. Her fever was well over a hundred, and she was barely conscious, slipping in and out of reality and not at all aware of or responsible for what she was saying. I had seen this behavior before in cancer patients, stabbing victims, and others traumatized into senselessness.

It is at these times that the real self comes out. I've heard these delirious ones swear at themselves, their families, and their God. I recalled hearing a pastor say that character is what you do when you are alone and are sure that you will not get caught. I remembered hearing someone who attended church regularly when at home say that he rarely went to church when visiting friends in other cities.

Let me insert a spiritual anomaly here for your consideration. It concerns someone that I knew many years ago, someone who is no longer in or near New York City. She was, when I met her, an extremely conservative Christian—very strict, very straight, extremely health conscious, and somewhat retiring. She was given to seasons of mental distress. During these times while hospitalized, she would don the tightest slacks, put on the most low-cut, revealing blouse, wear the reddest lipstick, and smoke nonstop. She would proposition the doctors, male nurses, orderlies—any male who happened to speak to her.

Her presentation was sensual and aggressive with the conversation centered on sex. I have no way of knowing what malfeasance of mind could account for this behavior. I would often visit her, and even as we prayed, her last words of prayer would be followed by some base comment or sensual innuendo. It was as though a demon had taken over; her countenance was frightening to see. These seasons came about once every fourteen months or so. There was

JULIET

no rhyme or reason to them, and once over, she had very little memory of her actions. She would, however, be possessed with an overwhelming sense of regret and remorse for something that she knew she had done but could not name nor identify.

The mind is a magnificent organ that Satan seeks to control and destroy. In point of fact, the arena for the cosmic battle between Christ and Satan is the mind. If the devil can destroy this wondrous tool through neglect, incorrect use, or drugs, he is satisfied. If one has no mind or a mind that is out of control or a mind that is warped and depraved through abuse, that soul is in jeopardy. Far too many in our world are willing to sell their minds or give them away.

We surrender our minds to the influence of friends, colleagues, rock, sports, and movie stars, to television, radio, and media. We allow so much of our world to occupy our thoughts and as such to shape and mold our lives. The conversation of so many today is simply a parody of the songs, slogans, jargon, and ideologies of pop culture. Original thought is a rare commodity. Sanctified thought is rarer still.

We rightly inveigh against the prostitute for selling his or her body, but perhaps the greatest sin is the selling, or outright giving away, of the mind. A mind, a character pawned or given away is an incredibly difficult thing to redeem, and even if one is successful at retrieval, it is usually in deplorable condition. I have learned when visiting hospital patients not to be too surprised on those occasions when a person's words are the product of fever and pain, a deteriorating body, and an uncensored tongue.

As Juliet slipped into semi-consciousness and began to ramble incoherently, I prepped my mind for a verbal barrage, the content of which I had no way of foretelling. What she said, she said loudly. In fact, so loudly that the doctors, nurses, attendants, and patients in the crowded, busy emergency room all but ceased their activities.

I WILL FEAR NO EVIL

That little lady on her stretcher began a homily that lasted for just short of twenty minutes. Her eyes were closed, her brow bathed in sweat and uncomfortably hot, even to the touch, her body convulsing occasionally, but somehow her mind, filled with the Spirit of God framed and formed words that literally poured from parched lips and stopped hardened hospital workers in their tracks.

"Nobody knows but Jesus," she began. "Nobody knows my joy and pain, my tears and my sorrow; nobody knows like Jesus." She spoke of her joy, her family, her love for her church and friends, the choir she sang in, her children. She quoted Scripture, the writings of Ellen White, and other material that she had read. She asked questions of no one in particular and answered them herself. She was loud, quite loud, but no one made a move to silence her. A nurse wiped the corners of her mouth and her forehead while fighting back her own tears.

I listened, and as I glanced around, I noticed that everyone was listening. A busy hospital emergency room in one of America's largest cities was brought to near standstill by the incoherent babbling of a fever-stricken patient who in her delirium did nothing but praise the name of Jesus.

Just as suddenly as the words began, they ceased, and Juliet slipped into exhausted slumber. The doctors, having completed their emergency procedures, prepared to take her to her room. The nurse suggested that we return home, as Juliet would sleep for some time.

As I looked at my watch, I was surprised to see that I had been at the hospital for over four hours, and her family for more than six. It was time to rest. Juliet would rest now, and I urged her mom and daughter to do the same. We had all been moved over the past few hours. We had taken an extended trip on an emotional roller coaster, and we were mentally drained. It was time to rest and regroup, as this would not be the last of such excursions we would take. My mind rehearsed Juliet's words as I walked to my car and drove home.

JULIET

I recalled looking into the tear-stained faces of many of the attendants in the emergency room. You could almost read the questions forming in their minds, "What did this girl do to deserve getting AIDS?"

It was a question that would be asked by many in the hospital and at church. My mind dredged up a conversation that had taken place over ten years earlier. A pastor was recounting an incident that had taken place while he was visiting a dying member. She was dying of liver failure and in much discomfort. As he walked down the hall toward her room, his ears were assaulted by some of the most vicious swearing he had ever heard. He thought to himself, "What kind of street urchin is spewing out that stream of filth?" To his surprise, it was coming from the room of, and the mouth of, the one he was going to visit. She, too, was semi-conscious, and her public patina was stripped. The cultured veneer had been removed by fever and disease, and in her distress her real self was exposed. Even her abject apology later could not erase what her pastor and everyone on the floor had heard. I recalled the text, "Out of the abundance of the heart the mouth speaketh" (Matthew 12:34). Perhaps, a modern translation might well read, "Under extreme stress, the real you shows itself." If that be the case, then we all saw the real Juliet that Friday morning. To no one's surprise it was as we suspected. The real Juliet was Juliet. The inner self was quite the same as the outer.

Someone once said that there are four kinds of people. The beautiful-ugly, the ugly-beautiful, the beautiful-beautiful, and the ugly-ugly. The beautiful-ugly are those persons who possess physical beauty. They are beautiful outside, but inside they are ugly. Their hearts and souls are ugly. Their beauty is only skin deep.

The ugly-beautiful are those individuals who are not much to look at physically. They may not be repulsive, but are not particularly attractive to the outward eye. Their beauty is within. Their heart, mind, and soul are sunlit and radiant. They are a joy to be around and are kind and considerate and generous in spirit.

The beautiful-beautiful are those persons who possess good looks and good characters. They look good and are good. What you see is, indeed, what you get, and it is good. Finally, the ugly-ugly are not much to look at and not much to be with—a horrible countenance matched by a horrible disposition, ugly out and ugly in.

Juliet had firmly established herself in the beautiful-beautiful category. Oddly enough, the sicker she got, the more beautiful she looked. That Friday morning Juliet, her body superheated by fever, sweat literally pouring from her brow, her hair a disheveled mess, was one of the most beautiful women I had ever seen.

I cannot count the number of times I visited Juliet in the hospital. I recall on one occasion walking in to see her mother-in-law leaning over her bed and speaking softly to her unconscious form. I stood outside, not wishing to interrupt a poignant moment. "I love you, Juliet," she intoned. "We all love you." She stroked her brow.

As she spoke, tears made their silent way down her cheeks and into the sheets. I waited a few more seconds before walking in. We exchanged greetings. "Juliet squeezed my hand," she said.

We prayed together, forming a circle with each of us holding one of Juliet's hands. Our prayer was interrupted by a nurse. She came in covered from head to toe with protective equipment. She shot an incredulous look at us as if to say, "Are you actually touching her?" We deciphered the words coming through her face mask as a request for us to leave. She drew the curtain and shut us out. After a while, she came out and walked silently by us. We concluded our prayer, took off our masks, and made our way to the door. "Next time, put on gloves," someone at the nurses' station shouted. We washed our hands, commented on the collective callousness of the health care system, and left.

Things got no better for Juliet. Even a valiant fighter has no

JULIET

chance against the death sentence that is AIDS. She fought long and hard, but in the end she lost the fight. She died peacefully, praising God and singing. Even her nurses were amazed. I am told by those with her during her last minutes that she ended her life exhibiting the same joy that had marked all her days.

I vividly recall her funeral. Although her family took the death hard, the remarks were all positive—recounting a life spent serving the church and society.

A young man came and asked to speak. I did not know him and had not seen him before. The family introduced him as a recent acquaintance of Juliet's. He was not scheduled to be on the program, but I felt impressed to allow him an opportunity to address the congregation.

During his remarks he revealed that he, too, was an AIDS patient. He had met Juliet in the hospital, and they had become instant friends. He said, "Juliet was an inspiration to us all. She would give Bible lessons to the patients on the ward. She was always talking about Jesus, and everybody loved her. A lot of us have accepted Christ because of Juliet. We will miss her on the ward."

Several of the nurses who attended her were also there. "She made an impact on my life," a spokesperson said. "Everyone loved her; she was such a little fighter."

I recall keeping a mental record of the number of times that I heard the word "fighter" used to describe Juliet. She certainly didn't look like a fighter. I remembered that once when we were feeding the homeless (she had volunteered for this also) she needed my help to lift what I thought was a fairly light case of pears. She laughed and said, "That's what pastors are for." No, she didn't look like a fighter, but in Juliet's case, looks were deceiving. Inside she was the fiercest of gladiators who, by her own testimony, was not afraid of very many things.

"She was the best mother you could have," her daughter said.

I WILL FEAR NO EVIL

"She was like a big sister. We could talk about anything. We all loved her, but God loved her best."

My mind went back to the last conversation I had with Juliet. "I love Jesus," she stated. "I'm OK with Him. I am not angry with God. He's been so good to me; everything is OK."

As we held hands to pray, I believed her. You could tell she knew what she was saying. I remember asking her once in the hospital, "Who is Jesus, Juliet?"

"He's mine, all mine," she said. Her lips continued to move, but the words were not audible. She closed her eyes and drifted off into sleep. She lived well and died well. And the promise for her is for all His fallen angels.

> Those who live for Him
> and die in Him
> *shall one day live forever.*

Juliet's life is, among other things, a testament to the power of one. Of the three principle characters in this book, she had the most impact on the day-to-day life of the church through her work. She was more centrally involved. She was into everything and doing so much and knew almost everyone. Her life was more public than that of Delissa or Tamara. Where these fought in silence, Juliet's struggle was a public one; everybody knew everything about her case.

She never made any attempt to conceal even the most intimate details of her failed marriage nor of her battle with AIDS. Perhaps it was the openness that drew so many to her. In Juliet, what you saw was what you got. She was extremely open and above board. If you asked a question, you got an answer. If the question was embarrassing, the answer probably would be, too. If you were so indiscreet as to ask for details, you got them, and if her frankness

JULIET

embarrassed you, that was the price you paid for asking.

I have had occasion in the ensuing years to compare and contrast elements of Delissa's and Juliet's respective stories. Both were women of exemplary faith and courage. Delissa, however, was terrified at the prospect of disclosure, whereas Juliet told all. Perhaps it was because Delissa was older. She was of a different generation. Her friends were more settled, more conservative, more apt to fear the unknown. Juliet was not, herself, free from the prejudice of others. There were some who backed off, some who kept a discreet distance, even some (very few, thank God) who chided me for embracing her before the church during Communion service, their words veiled as concern for my health.

These were the early days of HIV when much misinformation was afoot. We now know that you won't get AIDS from a handshake or hug or even a kiss on the cheek. If that were so, over half of the church would have been infected on the day that Juliet spoke to our church.

Juliet knew that some were turned off by her. She simply didn't care. She was too busy, too active. Those who loved her, loved her too well, and insulated her too securely to allow her to feel the icy draft of disdain. It was the coldness of these who kept their physical and emotional distance that justified for me Delissa's decision to remain silent.

How sad, I have often thought, that some stayed away for, had they only ventured to draw near, their cold hearts would have been warmed and softened by the love that Juliet radiated. How much we need each other in this world! The Juliets of the world need us, but in a less obvious but equally profound way, we need them. We need them to soften us, to help us to put our lives and our problems into perspective. We need them to move us from apathy to action, to disturb our quietude, and in that disturbing to force us to the realization that as Jesus said, "They that are whole need not a physician; but they that are sick," (Luke 5:31), and that sometimes the very best medicine is to be found in a handshake, a smile, a hug, or a kind word.

How easy it is to forget that when we help, we are helped ourselves. When we strive to be a blessing, we are, in turn, blessed. When we lift others, we, too, are lifted. It is an unalterable spiritual law. So many live impoverished spiritual lives because so much of their efforts for good or bad are concentrated on themselves. There is, I am convinced, a level of spiritual growth and maturity that can be reached only by serving others. God wants this for us. A person, a family, even a church that is concerned with itself only will die. It may, for some time, carry on the activities of a living organism, but in reality it is dead.

The crippled, the broken, those damaged by life are around us and in us. They need and, in a sense, deserve our help because we are they, they are us. None can tell you how to respond and what to do. That must come as a consequence of your compassion. But as God has given each of us gifts, all are called and equipped to do something in service to our fellow man outside and inside the church. Not to do so is to leave unexplored what might be the most fascinating, fulfilling, and rewarding aspects of our existence.

Juliet was public; Delissa was private. But both were in need. All around us are souls in need. Some will tell you; many, perhaps most, will not. We must look; we must keep our eyes open for the call for help however faint. And most importantly, we must be prepared to respond once the call is heard.

To those who are in trouble, your burden is to seek help. It's out there. There are kind, courteous, courageous Christians who will stand with you. There aren't as many as there should be, but please know that they are there. I have seen them in every church that I have pastored. You can spot them fairly easily—the real ones, the genuine ones, that is. They are helpers, nurturers, sympathizers.

JULIET

They cannot help themselves. It is their bequest from God; it is their nature; they are compulsive "carers."

Secrecy is a prison of sorts, but so is apathy. Apathy, if left untreated, is fatal. If there were more sympathy, there would be less secrecy. Less secrecy would allow love to be expressed and received more fully. That love would be our salvation, and those hurting would not be further wounded.

There are those who, by their actions, seem to state that they don't need anyone. Disbelieve your eyes! Everybody has needs, and those with needs are there for the benefit of those who seem to have none. Everybody needs somebody, and everybody needs to be needed. It is also true that everybody needs to be needed by somebody. And in the church I suspect that everybody needs to have somebody who is in need. The only thing commending us to God is our need, and it is in satisfying the needs of others that our lives and faith are affirmed.

The best church is one who, like Jesus, is touched by the pain and suffering of those of its own fellowship and of the wider community. Juliet forcefully showed us this. Helping and caring are as much a sermon as anything said in a pulpit during church service.

As we near the end of this age, the demands on our love will increase. We will have enough to share if we connect to, and continually draw from, the Source of all love. "He that loveth not, knoweth not God; for God is love" (1 John 4:8). Juliet's life affirmed that the person who loves enough can never be truly hurt or never be truly alone!

CHAPTER FIVE

Simon Says

In this chapter I would like to examine the life of a somewhat enigmatic New Testament character. It is my hope that in looking at this figure we can see and understand Heaven's love for the sinner and gain hope and strength for the battle that each of us must wage against ourselves.

The story concerns itself with the case of Simon the Leper, as he is known in Scripture. We are introduced to him in Luke 7:36, among other places in the Bible. Notice that in this instance, indeed, as in the majority of the times Simon is mentioned, he carries the cognomen "The Leper." His surname certainly was not "The Leper." We know that when baby Simon was taken to the synagogue in the days following his birth, his parents did not name him Simon the Leper. This Simon is identified by disease. It is not customary for individuals to be identified and earmarked by their infirmities.

In fact, in this age, obsessed as it is with political correctness, it is considered most déclassé to mention a person's disabilities. It is more socially acceptable to value a person for what he can do as opposed to devaluing him for what he cannot.

SIMON SAYS

Simon bar Jonah, to whom Jesus gave the name Peter, is of course, identified by his father's name—he is Simon bar (son of) Jonah. Simon the tanner is identified by his occupation. There is a parallel in Paul's mention of Alexander the coppersmith in 2 Timothy 4:14. Simon the Canaanite is identified by racial distinction. Simon of Cyrene, the black worthy from the north coast of Africa who assisted our Savior in carrying His cross, is, of course, identified by country of origin. None of these designations is particularly unusual or noteworthy. However, Simon the Leper is. Especially when one understands that this Simon was a ruler in Israel, a revered elder of the temple. Simon the Leper was none other than Simon the Pharisee, also called Simon of Bethany.

Simon was a member of the religio-political elite of the Jewish nation. The Pharisees commanded and demanded respect, even more than the priestly aristocratic Sadducees. But for all his earned respect and the excellence of his office, the name "Pharisee" meant little, for at some time after reaching the exalted position of a ruler in Israel, Simon was given a new name—a name that superseded all others. It didn't matter that he was a vaunted community leader or that he belonged to an exclusive ruling party. The new name erased and eclipsed all of that. From then on he was to be known as Simon the Leper.

To understand the ancient Hebrew mind set concerning leprosy and those afflicted with it, one must understand the theological and ecclesiastical implications of contracting the disease. A suspected leper was diagnosed as having the disease, not by a physician, but by the priest. The ancient Hebrews considered leprosy to be an affliction given by God to punish sinners. It was often referred to as the "finger of God" or the "stroke of God." When a person contracted leprosy his world dramatically and unalterably changed.

Lepers had to leave their families. Lepers had to leave their homes and move to pitiful leper colonies located away from those not likewise afflicted. Lepers could not attend public gatherings or celebrations. Lepers could not attend the synagogue. Lepers did not even have the comfort of pastoral, or rather rabbinical, presence, prayer, or counsel. A leper was as a dead man. Socially, spiritually, and in all meaningful respects, he was thought of and treated as a dead man. Lepers were feared, shunned, ostracized, treated with disdain, and scrupulously avoided. They were earmarked as those bereft of God. The thought seemed to be that if God had given them this punishment, then priests and people alike should have little use for them.

This theology was, perhaps, a perverted digest of the experiences of such Old Testament characters as Moses' sister Miriam (see Numbers 12) and King Uzziah (see 2 Chronicles 26) who were both struck with leprosy as a punishment for misdeeds. In the case of the latter, it was a disease from which he was never cured. Whether right or wrong, by Christ's time the notion that leprosy was a punishment for sin was firmly entrenched, taught by the priests and believed by the people.

Leprosy, horrible in its effects, disfiguring, debilitating, frightening to see, was, of course, incurable, and the scorn with which lepers were treated often made death a longed-for eventuality. This then is the background for the case of Simon the Leper. He comes to our attention because Jesus is visiting his home. This is a compelling statement, and the implications are far reaching.

A crowd is gathering. There is going to be a feast, a party, a social occasion at the house of Simon—Simon the Leper. Though it is not stated, we are forced to the conclusion that Simon must no longer be a leper. He simply couldn't be! Lepers weren't socialites. Lepers didn't invite guests over. Lepers didn't have parties. And even if they did, who would come? What good temple member would be seen in the company of a leper? We must, therefore, assume that Simon is a former leper—a healed leper, an ex-leper, if you will. In

SIMON SAYS

fact, it is his healing that occasions this gathering. Into this mix must be thrown the names of three notable characters—Mary, Martha, and Lazarus. Though only Simon's protagonist, Mary is germane to this story.

Let me pause here to deal with the great love of Jesus, which is demonstrated in His accepting this invitation to the Pharisee's house, particularly in the light of some information which will be discussed later. In detailing this story, I will draw from the inspired writings of the prophetic messenger, Ellen White, in her book, *The Desire of Ages*, that details the life and times of Jesus.

I would like to note that though we meet Simon healed of leprosy, his heart is neither cured nor cleansed of sin. Simon is not a converted, repentant individual. Quoting from the words of Mrs. White, "His character was not transformed; his principles were unchanged" (*The Desire of Ages,* 557). A great miracle had been wrought in the life of Simon of Bethany. However, this greatest of miracles, tantamount to the cancellation of a death sentence did nothing to change his unregenerate heart.

The point that I wish to emphasize here is that leprosy, though hated and despised by the Jews, was nothing to Jesus—not in the case of the ten lepers whose names aren't mentioned, or Simon. Men and women, boys and girls whom society would not wipe its shoes on, were loved, accepted, and blessed by Jesus.

Simon is a celebrity. His name gets mentioned. The ten lepers are what would be described as common men, and their names are not mentioned. All, however, receive the same treatment from Jesus—they get healed. It is need and faith that commends us to Christ, not fame or finances. There are no celebrities in heaven, nor is there anyone who is beneath Heaven's notice. Call! He hears! Volume isn't important. Even if your vocal cords never make a sound, I guarantee (and more importantly, He does too) that the Lord will hear you.

I WILL FEAR NO EVIL

There are diseases today that are viewed in much the same way as leprosy was in Christ's time. There are those who say that these diseases are a judgment from God. Some have said that persons contracting these diseases are beneath contempt. Besides being untrue, these statements are unbiblical and unnecessarily cruel to those contracting the disease through no malfeasance of their own.

Jesus did not fear leprosy. He does not fear AIDS, cancer, heroine, crack, STDs. Even if the world rejects those persons afflicted by these things, even if every man, woman, boy, or girl turns from them, Jesus never will. It is an old, shopworn phrase, but it remains very true—"Christ hates the sin, but loves the sinner." Christ said, "Him that cometh to me I will in no wise cast out" (John 6:37). There is no sin that cannot be forgiven. There is no malady that cannot be healed. God does what He wills because He is sovereign. He chose to heal Simon with no recorded profession of faith. Why? Because He is God, and it is within the purview and power of God to know what will happen in the future. Simon was a sinner, but Jesus came to save sinners!

If you are a sinner (and all have sinned), Jesus is for you! The nature of your sin is immaterial; it is the nature of the Savior that is important.

Simon was a leader—a man looked up to by others, and yet he was as divorced from God as the worst heathen. He was, in effect, a hypocrite, and yet Simon, saddled as he was with a load of sinful baggage, was loved by Jesus. Jesus loved him. Jesus healed him, and now Jesus accepts his invitation to dinner. Jesus is seated at a table between Lazarus, recently raised from the dead, and Simon, recently healed from a disease that rendered him as good as dead. This is the blessed reality for all who have sinned and who are suffering. Jesus, our Lord, will come and sup with you and sit with you and be your Friend.

There now begins to unfold a series of events, the true scope of which space will not allow me to examine. They are initiated by the

SIMON SAYS

actions of Mary, the younger of Lazarus's two sisters. Mary, whose sins had been forgiven by Jesus and whose love for Him was great. We are not made privy to the nature of her sins, and they do not matter. The salient fact here is that her sins were forgiven.

In gratitude she slips to the feet of Jesus, opens a box of perfumed ointment, and anoints his feet, drying them with her hair. Her secret act of love and homage is soon made public as the scent of the ointment broadcasts her activities throughout the house.

Immediately the hearts and minds and mouths of the evil-hearted are stirred to action. Some whisper, some gossip, some consider silently, some express their feelings. Judas creates a self-revealing scene, castigating both Christ and Mary. Simon, who does not speak, finds recourse in the machinations of his own evil heart. His thought process is best stated in Luke 7:39—" 'If this man (Jesus) were a prophet, he would have known who and what sort of woman this is who is touching him' " (RSV). He adds, thinking to himself, " 'for she is a sinner.' "

I have often felt that one of the reasons that so many in the Christian community can be so haughty, self-righteous, and judgmental is that they forget that they, too, are sinners! I am not asking that we excuse sin or brush by it lightly. I understand and accept the Lord's call and challenge for clean, Spirit-led, godly living. However, I am pleading that when we find ourselves dealing with those caught in sin, particularly those who are penitent, we must be kind, conciliatory, and redemptive, in short, Christlike. It is never ever wrong to be kind, loving, and uplifting.

Jesus knew what was transpiring within Simon's heart. Christ was keenly aware of the nature of the head, heart, and soul of the man seated next to Him. Simon, too, was a sinner. Mary was a forgiven sinner, and yet Simon, in his pride and prejudice, could not imagine himself in the same spiritual boat as she.

This is made more graphic when one considers this statement:

I WILL FEAR NO EVIL

"Simon had led into sin the woman he now despised. She had been deeply wronged by him" (*The Desire of Ages,* 566). Again, we are not made privy to the nature of the assignations between Simon and Mary. Suffice it to say, whatever her sins may have been, Simon had led her into them. Surely he could speak of what manner of woman she was, because whatever she was, he had had a hand in making her that way. He would not touch her in public and would think ill of Jesus for doing so. He did, however, touch her in private. All of this was known to Jesus. He knew Simon's history and He knew Mary's.

Christ could have asserted His prerogative to expose Simon's hypocrisy before his guests. Jesus could have seized this opportunity to publicly embarrass and permanently destroy Simon's credibility in his own home in front of his own friends at his own party. An argument could be made that this proud legalistic, self-righteous hypocrite deserved to be royally dressed down by Jesus. As I have mentioned elsewhere in this book, there are some who take a perverse delight in seeing the mighty fall. When Jim Bakker and Jimmy Swaggert fell, there were those who openly rejoiced, as though the fall of these two men legitimized their own sins. Too often, when we hear of a preacher's trouble, we talk and laugh and whisper and gloat and sometimes embellish when we should be weeping and praying for them and for ourselves. I am constrained to say again that when a wounded soul falls into spiritual disrepair, we must not seek to shut him off from the love of Christ. We cannot make light of the sin, but we dare not crush what hope remains.

The Communication Department of the General Conference has adopted the transmission of hope as its theme for the image of the world church. Jesus is the answer, and among the many blessings He offers to a distressed world is hope.

There is precious little hope left in this world. The streets, the houses, the hospitals are gorged with people who have no hope, and

SIMON SAYS

when someone falls into sin or is caught in sin they will never recover if they have no hope. Jesus, our glorious Savior, is a Lord of love and hope. This is the essence of the burden to be borne by those who designate themselves the followers of Christ.

So then, it is most noteworthy that Jesus chose not to publicly unmask Simon. Instead, He couched His chastening in the words of a parable that concerned two debtors. Having stated the parable, He asked Simon for a ruling on the matter. Simon gave Christ the answer He sought, and in doing so, he began to see himself in a new light. Additional words by Jesus began to shine increased light into the dark recesses of Simon's heart. His response is again best stated by Mrs. White: "Simon was touched by the kindness of Jesus in not rebuking him before his guests. He had not been treated as he desired Mary to be treated. He saw that Jesus did not wish to expose his guilt to others, but sought by a true statement of the case, to convince his mind and by pitying kindness to subdue his heart" (*The Desire of Ages*, 567).

In short, if Jesus had, in New York City street jargon, "busted him" (exposed him), He would have lost him. Jesus did not excuse Simon's sin. In fact, the parable was designed to show Simon that his sin was greater than Mary's.

Christians ought ever to keep in mind that the sins of pride, hypocrisy, and self-righteousness are especially galling to the Lord, incredibly difficult to self-diagnose, and particularly tough to get rid of. These sins were the pillars of Simon's life, but Christ's actions, like a mighty, spiritual Sampson, pulled down those pillars, and Simon's heart and world were broken.

Ellen White states, "His pride was humbled, he repented and the proud Pharisee became a lowly, self-sacrificing disciple" (*The Desire of Ages*, 568).

It was love that conquered. That quality that is in such incredibly short supply. That element that costs nothing to give and yet pays such handsome dividends. It was then, and remains, the an-

I WILL FEAR NO EVIL

swer to the ills, prejudices, and bigotry of our world. It is illogical and unreasonable that we apply it so sparingly.

On two occasions I have heard well-meaning but incredibly myopic, ministers state from the pulpit: What do AIDS and drugs have to do with Christians? This supposedly rhetorical question hurt and disturbed me. Christians don't live in a vacuum. Some have spouses that are non-Christian. Some have close friends, children, parents, siblings, neighbors who are touched by all that touches humanity. Being a Christian does not magically remove you from the real world, and it is unjust, unfair, irresponsible, and, to my mind, a little naive to think otherwise. No one wants pain. We need to spend our lives alleviating pain. Christ's way is still the best way, and His methodology is sorely needed in our world today. It is never wrong to forgive. The Lord's prayer intones, "Forgive us our debts, as we forgive our debtors" (Matthew 6:12). Those who never forgive and who walk with cold, callous stares; who choose not to speak to others or to ignore or to avoid, are not kind, are not actuated by Christ, and in fact, are fools, because ultimately, the only persons they are hurting are themselves. If Jesus can save the Simons and the Peters and the Davids and the Solomons of this world, then rest assured, He can and will save you and me.

There is no reality more sure and certain in this world than the truth that the Lord stands willing and able to deliver you. Two texts come to mind: "A bruised reed He will not break, and smoking flax He will not quench; He will bring forth justice for truth" (Isaiah 42:3, NKJV).

And this one: " 'All that the Father gives Me will come to Me, and the one who comes to Me I will by no means cast out' " (John 6:37, NKJV). What wonderful promises! Take them to the bank! Take them to your friends! Take them to heart!

All we have is each other and Jesus. I need you—you need me. With all my faults and failures, I know that Jesus will accept me. Will you?

I Will Fear No Evil

CHAPTER SIX

Ministering to the Fallen

The cities. I often wonder what will become of the cities. An associate of mine expressed his desire to serve somewhere, anywhere, other than New York City. "It's not the people," he moaned, "it's the life, city life." Sadly, his feelings are shared by many who find coping with city pressure almost intolerable. The city pulls from you; it wears on you; it fights and impedes you. You can live at peace with it; you can, with effort and caution, manage an uneasy détente; but it is a mistake to ever consider it your friend. It takes a special mind-set to live and work in the city.

In this section I want to send a call, or better, to plead not only with those of my colleagues in the ministry, but to all of those involved in counseling, training, teaching, and guidance. Allow me, please, to plead for a new order of ministry, a modification in the way we deal with the people and problems of the city. A ministry that prizes conciliation over condemnation, a ministerial posture that is keenly aware of the law, one that knows the *dos* and *don'ts* and that in no way apologizes for the values and regulations inherent in the law, and yet seeks a ministry that values love over law and

I WILL FEAR NO EVIL

life over death. When you are dealing with life, there must be more than pure law.

Far too often men and women who find themselves in trouble are forced to suffer silently or to have their fainting spirits evaporate in the loveless desert of accusatory finger pointing prevalent among far too many so-called Christians. The clergy is not immune. On the contrary, it is oftentimes in the forefront of the crowd that appears all too ready to shoot its wounded. How sad, that we who know the remedy for all spiritual maladies seem so reticent to apply it. When one of our fellows breaks down or falls too far behind, our solution is: "Shoot him! Put him out of his misery!"

It seems as though in our rush to get to heaven we have little time to keep track of stragglers and strays. Even on occasions when we attempt healing, it often comes long after the obligatory "I told you so;" "You are going to hell if you don't stop;" or "What's the matter with you?" aided and abetted by the skillful, almost surgical, application of a major league guilt trip—"Think of what this is going to do to your mother or your wife or husband or children or the church." We'll trot out any and every significant other, as long as the mention of the name will make the offending sinner feel bad—hopefully bad enough to change.

As a corporate Christian community, we have yet to master the art of placing a soft cushion beneath a falling victim. Rather, we watch intently to see if, having hit the pavement, they bounce back. If they do, we rejoice and praise the Lord; if not, bang, bang, you're dead! The Bible is, I have found, a most wondrous tool. Its texture changes according to the one wielding it. In the loving hands of a Christian practitioner, it is soft and inviting, cozy and warm, sweet and endearing. In the hands of a judgmental legalist, it becomes a rod of iron, a cudgel to bludgeon the heads of the guilty and the fallen. It is a knife to open the wrists of those caught in their sins. Sometimes we do the lacerating ourselves; at other times, in our

MINISTERING TO THE FALLEN

cowardice, we simply leave the knife nearby so that the ailing patient may slash his own wrists and put himself out of his misery away from our eyes.

Gentlemen and ladies, may I plead for compassion in all our dealings? May I assert that people are worth more than things? That true love, though a rare commodity, is above all things? It is the one thing, even in New York City, that cannot be stolen and indeed is best when given away.

Spiritual flagellation of a back already beaten raw by life, is akin to the medieval practice of putting leeches on sick patients to draw out the bad blood. The practice draws from them the very substance so needed to sustain life. I believe with all my heart that it is the very real fear of additional, unnecessary, self-righteous bloodletting that keeps so many of the spiritually wounded at bay. When I am bleeding, I do not need a razor blade; I need a bandage.

I feel that it should be stated that I am not going soft on sin. There is far too much of that today. Pastors, churches, entire denominations are busily restructuring their credal foundations to accommodate all manner of evil. Some have sacrificed conscience on the altar of popularity, fearing to take a stand that would result in decreased membership. Christ still constrains us to call sin by its right name and to declare unstintingly that wrong is still wrong. But even when we must apply the iodine of truth to an open wound, we must stay there to spiritually blow softly on the cut, in order to make the healing as painless as possible and do all in our power to make sure that the patient does not die.

Following are two short stories. They are meant to cause you to think and, hopefully, to examine yourself.

The first concerns a young lady whom I will call Dawn—a pretty, petite, shy seventeen-year-old. Dawn grew up in a Christian home, coddled, fawned over, overprotected, but not spoiled. She was bright, inquisitive, and amazingly innocent and naive for a na-

I WILL FEAR NO EVIL

tive New Yorker. Her first real experience with boys turned out to be traumatic.

Before finishing her story I must tell you about her father, the classic, posturing, pompous Pharisee. He was a Christian who wore his religion like an arrogant badge. A well-dressed pseudo-sophisticated know-it-all for whom the most irritating facet of life was that he was not given due credit for the vast storehouse of knowledge he felt he possessed. His goal in life seemed to be keeping his personal Christian reputation spotless. I cannot, dare not, say that he was all bad. He possessed a number of admirable qualities. He simply was who he was, and at times that took some getting used to. His wife, a demure, meditative follower, seldom questioned his pretensions.

Dawn, their daughter, kept herself in line. First, because her hovering parents never allowed her an opportunity to do otherwise. Second, because her many church and after-school activities occupied much of her time. Third, because of the most inordinate fear of what her peacock of a father would do if she ever "let him down."

But in spite of all this, somehow Dawn had gotten herself in trouble, and a friend came to me stating that Dawn wanted to speak with me, but that I had to promise not to tell anyone. Not wanting to get into a trap concerning someone so young, I refused to promise to keep the secret. Two weeks later the friend came again stating that Dawn was in *serious* trouble and that she had to talk, but that I had to promise not to tell. Again I refused. A month passed, and the friend returned stating that Dawn was in real trouble and that it was a "sex thing" and that I simply had to talk to her. I had been telling the friend to have Dawn speak to her father, but Dawn would not. Instead she ran away from home. The friend knew where she was and told me that Dawn would speak to me, but the condition was the same. I could not tell anyone. The church knew that she had run away but only I knew why. I decided that enough was enough and that I would accept Dawn's condition. We met at a place of her choosing, and she unfolded the following story.

She had met a guy at school, tall, handsome, slick, nineteen years old, non-Christian, and sexually active. This latter aspect of his life was unknown until some months later. His smooth talk and insistence garnered for him one liaison with Dawn. One was all that was necessary. She came to me riddled with shame and guilt. Her first time with a boy was not at all as she had pictured it. No caressing, no caring, no conversation, and no love. The memories were not fine. Groping insistence, hurrying, pain, and bleeding was what she took from her first experience with a boy. She was manipulated and coerced by someone who knew what he wanted and how to get it, and in her naivete she was unable to protect herself or resist. The following days found her filled with regret, self-pity, loneliness, and one additional thing—venereal disease. Not AIDS, thank God, but certainly one of the numerous STDs afflicting those who have multiple sexual partners or those who are with those who do.

She had a rash and an itch, and she felt alone and afraid. She couldn't tell her mother because "she would just die." She also refused to tell her father who, she insisted, would "kill me and even then wouldn't forgive me!" She was so uncomfortable that she could barely sit still. What was I, her pastor, to do? What would you do?

Here I was listening to Dawn telling me that she had VD and that her parents had no idea—and I had given my word not to tell a soul. Dawn's only solace lay in this promise extracted from me that I would remain silent. She asked for my word again before she began. I had given my word, and her revelation was based on her belief that the person she was speaking to was trustworthy. She told me everything, fully believing that nothing would ever be told to anyone, least of all her family.

Reverberating in my mind was the knowledge that Dawn's characterization of her parents was accurate. I could almost envision her enraged father's hands around her throat upon receiving the news of her unchaste activity. I kept my word and kept my silence. I contacted some pastoral friends and gave them a "what if . . ." hypothetical case. I was told where to go and who to see. Dawn and I made a date to go to the public health center.

It was an eye-opening experience. The vast majority of women there, some astonishingly young, were prostitutes. The overworked, aggravated doctors and nurses had little time for bedside manner. I felt patently uncomfortable as I entered, wearing a three-piece suit, with Dawn trailing along sheepishly. I wondered if they thought that I was her pimp or consort. I really wished that I had dressed down.

The doctor called her by number. She went in, and I waited nervously. I used the time to make some decisions. If this was serious, I would have to tell her parents. I knew that I was close to the edge on this one, and I had to extricate, or at least protect, myself. But then I was forced to define the word "serious." Did "serious" mean life-threatening? Did it mean something that Dawn might carry as a physical or emotional scar for the rest of her life? Dawn was close to her eighteenth birthday, but she was still technically a minor. In truth, the whole situation was serious and I was running the risk of getting into real trouble.

She returned in a few minutes wearing a partial smile. "It's not serious," she said, "they gave me a shot, and I paid them. I'll be OK." On the way home she recounted the disdain with which the doctor had treated her, mumbling something about whores, and being particularly insensitive as he examined her. The experience was enough. The forty or so women and men in the waiting room were graphic evidence of what can happen when you live a certain way. Dawn pledged in my presence that this first time would be her last. Her resolve was strengthened when, at the doctor's insistence, she informed her ex-boyfriend that he should see a doctor and

MINISTERING TO THE FALLEN

received for her trouble an incredibly hard slap in the face.

It has been years since this incident. As far as I know, Dawn has been true to her word. She has lived a model Christian life and has finished college. I never told. Was I wrong? Did I show love and compassion or stupidity? Did I unnecessarily jeopardize my position, my career? Was I wise or a fool? Did I help her or hurt her? Was I a pastor or a pimp? Would you have done otherwise? What rules would you use to make your determination? Whose rights demand precedence, Dawn's or her parents?

Do even minors have rights? Should a seventeen-year-old be allowed to have such a secret? What kind of secrets are your young people carrying, and perhaps of cardinal importance, why are there secrets at all? Why can they not tell someone—tell you? Are you quite sure what your actions would have been in this case? Do you have a one-size-fits-all answer for this type of case—perhaps, something you read in a book or something that a scholarly professor or respected adult once told you. Is this kind of thing easy? If you think so, please think again! I have mentioned this case in workshops that I give at churches and have had many, mostly young people, say that I did well, while others, mostly parents, are quite divided. I have even had one young lady tell me of a similar experience that she had to go through—though, sadly, she had to do so alone.

The second and last story is not mine. I cannot verify its authenticity, and it was told to me so many years ago that I cannot remember its author. I have used it in sensitivity sessions and commend it to you for thought.

A young, unmarried lady was the mother of a single daughter, six years old. When she began attending church she was living with the child's father. This fact was fairly well-known. The lady in question had lived a fast life but then decided to give that life to Christ. She moved out of the apartment and changed her lifestyle. She was baptized into the church and immediately began working for the cause she had embraced. In two short years she became a model Christian. She began to earn the love and respect of her fellow members.

Sadly, in her third year it became obvious that she was pregnant again. She was still unmarried, and that was not good. Tongues began to wag; she was openly castigated. She was called a tramp, and everyone assumed that she had returned to her old ways, fornicating and living in sin. Everyone was disappointed, and the church leaders felt that she should be disciplined for disgracing herself and her church.

The pastor in a moment of mercy asked to be allowed to meet with her before the officers summarily dismissed her without a hearing. During his consultation with her, she told the following story.

She said that when she came to Christ, she did so fully. She ended her relationship with her boyfriend, as he did not want to marry her. As a Christian she still spoke with him from time to time and allowed him to periodically visit his daughter, the child that she had borne for him.

On one occasion, three months earlier, he came to visit in a drunken state. He was abusive and unruly. When he discovered that the daughter was sleeping soundly, he forced his attentions on her in an attempt to revive old times. When she refused his advances, he slapped her and raped her. Ashamed and fearful she said nothing, but put the incident behind her. She had found out only recently that she was pregnant! She begged for mercy, claiming that this pregnancy was not the result of a sinful liaison, but the result of a vicious, violent act by a jilted ex-lover.

The church officers were unsympathetic. They saw the story as a ruse—a not-too-clever concoction cooked up to cover a sinful slip-up. They were not postured to extend mercy. They were "not fools"; they were "not born yesterday"; and they "did not just come

MINISTERING TO THE FALLEN

off the boat." They had "seen this kind of thing before"; they were not, and would not be, taken in. The only one who believed her story was the pastor. He stood unhesitatingly behind her.

Do you believe her story? What actions would you take? What if you were the only one who believed her? What if the church board voted that she was lying? Can truth be determined by majority vote? What stand should you take? What if the church board voted against her, but she really was telling the truth? If she is lying, who is she really lying to? Whose job is it to make sure that she is not?

Perhaps the answers to those questions say more about who you are and what you believe than all the song singing, prayer praying, sermon preaching, and good-deed doing that you perform. Perhaps you are afraid to answer. Worse still, maybe you feel that the answer is easy and that you would solve this in an instant. Perhaps, like me, you would pray much, act slowly, and err on the side of mercy. Maybe you would leave the Bible within reach, praying that the situation would resolve itself.

A text comes to mind that has to do with our treatment of our fellow human beings: "Be kindly affectioned one to another with brotherly love; in honour, preferring one another." (Romans 12:10). I told this story to a group of pastors at a meeting some time ago. Almost universally they agreed to believe the story and said that they would stand with her. When the session was over, a colleague came to me in private and said, "It's real easy to be brave and sure when the problem is only on paper. It's a lot tougher when it's your church and your board and your members and your ministry on the line." He admitted that he simply didn't know what he would do. I'd still be praying, he said.

That's not a bad idea!

I Will Fear No Evil

CHAPTER SEVEN

Stopping the Fall

In this chapter I want to speak to those who might be entangled in self-destructive, addictive behavior, be it drugs, promiscuity, music (yes, music can be very destructive and addictive), adultery, or any of the thousand and one sinful habits that we can be saddled with. The answer to these addictive behaviors, of course, is Jesus—better stated, Jesus and you. There is a way to free yourself, truly and fully and permanently!

"Pure religion has to do with the will." These words were penned by a great prophetic messenger, Ellen G. White, in the latter part of the nineteenth century. I firmly believe that the way to break the hold that negative, addictive behavior has on a falling individual is the correct use of the will in concert with divine assistance. The key lies in how the will is used. Failure comes not because the will is too weak, but because our admittedly weak wills are misapplied.

When one uses his own will to control or eliminate habits, feelings, or urges that have, over a period of time and through repeated indulgence, become part of his nature, that individual is

STOPPING THE FALL

doomed to failure. Any success will be only temporary since self is fighting self. There will be times when our willpower is stronger than self and occasions when it is weaker than self. Consequently, self will lose out to self with unpredictable regularity. It other words, there will be times when your desire to be free of a bad habit will overrule, and you will be able to stop through the force and exercise of your will. Notwithstanding, there will also be times when the strength of the bad habit will overrule your desire to be free, because the habit is also part of you. The longer the habit has been with you and the more times it has been repeated, the greater a part of you it is.

There are those who divide human nature into the positive, or higher self and the negative, or lower self. These designations are of little pragmatic value because, first, there is debate over what constitutes the negative nature and, secondly, and perhaps more importantly, the habit, be it positive or negative, is still part of self. It matters not so much if the behavior is considered positive or negative. The fact is that what you are dealing with is part of you, a facet of your own nature. If the only weapon employed to fight self is self, you are defeated before you begin.

In short, any activity that you engage in becomes part of you. It fuses with your mind, your body, and your soul. If it is something that is deeply ingrained in you or something that you have indulged in for a particularly long period of time, then it will take more than your will to release you from it because your will, which is part of you, is fighting this habit, which is now also a part of you. Additionally, if you are like so many today who have no legacy of self-discipline, self-denial, or self-control, you will find it nearly impossible to make the necessary corrections in your life.

For example, most young people today have grown up in the "beat" generation. Their music, from rhythm and blues, to rap, to rock, to gospel is heavily beat-oriented. Many will tell you that they

I WILL FEAR NO EVIL

just like it, but if the truth be told, it is more than that. The truth is that they are slaves to it.

The beat is now part of them, and music possessing no accentuated beat is not really enjoyed, it is merely tolerated. Many times it is rejected outright. Listening to and picking up the beat is the way they approach music. If you could get one to try and turn his back totally on any music with an accentuated beat that young person would find the task almost impossible. He might succeed for a matter of days or weeks but to ask him to make it a lifestyle change would be to saddle him with an almost superhuman task. This is so because his only weapon would be his will, and he is battling something that is as much a part of him as is his will.

The power that anything has over a person is directly proportional to the effort it takes for that person to volitionally withdraw from it. The reason that you need Jesus is because without Him you stand no real chance. A genuine understanding of your own weakness is prerequisite to your healing.

All of us were born in sin and shaped in iniquity. We all have faults—some more visible than others. But even those individuals who appear to skip through life without a care, have problems. Ultimately, it matters not so much what one's sin is because the wages of all sin is death.

The answer to all sin is the same—Jesus. You may stop doing a thing by sheer force of will, but you can be victorious over it only through the blood of, the presence of, and the power of, Jesus.

You may be one of the minority of individuals whom the Lord chooses to free from a habit or sin in one miraculous instant. The odds are that this will not be your fate for a number of biblically sound and supported reasons. I am not a believer in the "name it, claim it" brand of religion that is purveyed by so many today. We can ask for healing, a cure, or a miraculous delivery from sin. The Lord, who is sovereign, may answer in one of three ways: "Yes,"

STOPPING THE FALL

"No," or "Not now." Our faith in Him does not and cannot override, His ability to answer as He chooses. Faith does not force God's hand.

Most of us walk into sin with our eyes wide open. My experience has confirmed the reality that most of us will have to walk out of sin one step at a time. Indeed, it is the battle hard fought and won, that is most respected. If we could, with a snap of the finger or a quick prayer, completely free ourselves from the effects of sinful acts and habits, there would be that much less of a deterrent to engage in them. Anything worth having in life is worth effort. This includes freedom from sin.

The development of character allows for few shortcuts. A fine, cultured Christian life is the product of daily battles with self. Certain habits and traits seem so deep-rooted that we see no way to rid ourselves of them. But the good news is that with Jesus, all things are possible.

We are not left to fight alone or in our own strength. Heaven has promised to stand by our side. When we fight, Omnipotence fights with us. Easy? No, it is certainly not easy. Possible? Oh yes, very much so. All things are possible with Jesus. Even when we fall we must not give up on ourselves. Jesus never does. He is committed to our success. The question is: Are we? If there is one fact proven over and over in the Bible and in life, it is that Christ can and does make changes. Let no one fool you. Nothing worth having in this life comes without cost, and this fact goes double for character development.

To paraphrase a statement by Ellen White, the effort must be commensurate with the prize sought. A great prize will be obtained only through the expenditure of great effort. I am counseling someone now who spends most of his time asking, "Why me?" This is fruitless, counterproductive, and a waste of time. That may sound harsh, but it is quite true. Who knows why he faces a particular difficult situation? Suffice it to say that everybody has things to overcome. If salvation came in a can, everybody would have it. The fact is that we will be saved through surrender, prayer, faith, trust, and stern constant battles with self. Get beyond the "Why me?" The fact is that it *is* you, and now that that's established, where do you go from here? Answer to Jesus.

You are in for a fight. You are fighting the strongest, cleverest, most persistent and well-armed foe you will ever face. You are fighting yourself. Do not fight alone. Do not suffer in silence. Find someone that you can talk to, someone that you can trust. Someone who can carry and share your burdens. Perhaps, more importantly, someone who will tell you the truth.

Remember, everyone that tells you how good you are and who showers you with compliments and praise is not necessarily your friend. And everyone that speaks sharply to you, puts you in your place, and reminds you that the sun does not rise and set around you is not necessarily your enemy.

When you are falling, the one thing you need most is the truth. Lies are not therapeutic. They are counterproductive. Even if you are lying to yourself, the truth must be told.

Allow me to suggest that the world today is characterized by addiction. There is, I believe, a certain addiction even in adrenaline. People today have become addicted to the rush, the feeling of adrenaline released into their systems. Consequently, there is a certain mind set that constantly seeks pleasure and thrills. Television and motion pictures must be more action oriented or more sexually explicit or more violent in order to satiate the thrill-seeking masses. The world has a desire to live at a fever pace and pitch and is soon bored with quiet solitude. The music has to be louder, the party more risque, the clothing racier. New fads and fancies are concocted daily in an effort to keep pace with the jaded appetite of a society that is addicted to sensory stimulation.

STOPPING THE FALL

Addiction, among other things, leads to our fall. We investigate, experiment with, and soon become addicted to certain activities, which quickly become our master. Under the control of these vices, we begin an inexorable downward spiral, the terminus of which is our own moral and spiritual dissolution. Oftentimes this process ends in concomitant physical dissipation and death. In short, the thing that results in our spiritual ruin usually destroys our body as well.

All is not grim, though. There is good news. It is found in the sentiments of Jesus. As long as life lasts, hope lasts. You can make changes.

Alcoholics Anonymous has found that by appealing to the aid of a "higher power" one can beat alcohol addiction. I believe that this is the way to success when dealing with sin. I choose, however, to name the higher power. His name is Jesus. He is an inexhaustible Source of strength to those in need. The key to your success is tapping into that Power Source.

Here's one way: You must focus your energies, not on the sin, fault, or habit. This is of utmost importance. It also goes against the grain of much of the counsel floating around today. Your object is to move beyond the sin, not focus on it. For example, let's use cocaine addiction. First, avail yourself of whatever professional medical assistance is available to you. It is important that the best possible medical care be secured. You must understand that most medical care, however, will be aimed at the physical aspect of addiction. The mental, moral, and spiritual aspects of addiction will have to be handled by you. Doctors have no drugs for mind, soul, and spirit. That prescription must come from the Divine Physician.

Next, you must train what will you have on getting closer to Christ. Discipline yourself to make time for Bible reading and prayer. Begin each day with a prayer and consecrate yourself to God for that day (everything is accomplished on a one-day basis). Work in increments of one day. Tomorrow must be left to tomorrow. You must understand that your strength to overcome comes as a consequence of a vital, living relationship with Jesus.

If you walk on the beach, you will inevitably get sand in your shoes. If you walk with Jesus, you will inevitably get Him into your heart. And like sand in the shoe, Jesus in the heart is extremely tough to get out. Just when you think you are free of it, you find that there is a little left and that you cannot move comfortably until you deal with it. If you attempt to proceed, you find that it cannot be ignored. It is there affecting your every step, altering both your cadence and your gait. If you are trying to run with the world, you will find it a constant irritant. That is just how Jesus is—hard-headed, persistent, determined to love us. He does not let go easily. He takes an awful lot of abuse from the human family. Thank God, Jesus is equal to the challenge.

So then, focus on Jesus, not the problem. This enables you to get mentally and spiritually away from and beyond the problem. Although at this point you are probably still emotionally, mentally, and physically hooked (such as is the case with all sin addiction), one segment of your complex nature has moved to another plane. Some would counsel you to use your strength to resist committing the infraction, that is, whenever the urge comes, just concentrate on not doing it. This, I repeat, is futile. Sooner or later you will be overcome by your will, and you will have a relapse.

Additionally, and perhaps more importantly, if you are using your will to concentrate on a problem, you are stuck at that problem. To concentrate on a thing, either to do it or not, holds you at that point in your journey. It's always on your mind. It's always in your heart. You are constantly thinking about it. You are not putting it behind you. It is ever before you, like a flag, a banner, a barrier. As long as you concentrate on it, you will never get the

STOPPING THE FALL

victory over it, be free of it, or put it behind you. You are stuck there on it, and you must get "by it." The only way is by focusing, not on "it," but on something or someone who can take your mind and heart to another place.

Let me again emphasize that using the will to refrain from committing an act, is an exercise in futility. I am not saying not to use your will at all. You must do that, but your will alone, when used to resist something, is simply not enough. There are times when you will have to call upon a determined will for short-term resistance. In the long run, your own will must have assistance. Pro-action is better than reaction; running to Jesus is better than running from sin; trying to do something is better than trying not to do something.

I need to add that it is not enough to focus on another human being, even a loving spouse or relative. First, each of us has our own problems and cannot provide the continual, constant, positive input necessary. Each of us has good days and bad ones, and no matter how sincere, we cannot always be there for each other. Second, changes must be made, not to please others, but to improve ourselves for our own good. One does not cease smoking crack because his mom nags him or even because it is killing him. But he can, and will, stop when his love for Christ replaces the crack addiction with love, freedom, the power and desire to say "No!" This comes from within. Jesus is no mere cosmetologist. His concern goes far beyond the exterior. He is a skillful heart Surgeon who exchanges new hearts and new lives for old ones.

Allow me to define victory as it has been used here. Sin has dominion over us. That is to say, it affects the present life and also our future life. The Bible says that "the wages of sin is death" (Romans 6:23), so the unconfessed sin ruins our life now and disqualifies us for a heavenly afterlife. If by sheer force of will, we stop sinning, we have helped ourselves in this life. The problem is that

I WILL FEAR NO EVIL

even if we never again sin, we are still guilty of past sins. Those past sins will keep us out of heaven if left unconfessed and unforgiven. So then, those past sins still have "dominion" over us, as they will determine where we will spend eternity. The only way to get them blotted out is through Jesus.

When we come to Christ, He forgives and forgets. We then are out from under the condemnation of past sins; we are, in effect, victorious over sin. It is erased from our past, removed from our present, and has no bearing on how we spend eternity. We can take care of today and perhaps tomorrow, but Jesus is Lord of our past. Once lived, I can do nothing about yesterday. Jesus can!

This is important because your yesterdays affect your tomorrows. Your tomorrows affect your forever.

Let me return to my thesis, for this is important. In our battle with self, the only sure weapon is Christ. It is His power, His strength, that will make us victorious. So, when the urge to do cocaine comes, rather than focusing on the drug, saying, "I will not, I will not," you focus on Jesus, saying, "I will, I will, I will serve Jesus." Rather than the negative focus on not doing the drugs, you use the positive focus on serving Jesus. It is also important that you apply Christ at the point of attack. Let me repeat—apply Christ at the point of attack.

It is useless to pray in the morning in your home for the strength of Jesus and leave it there. YOU MUST APPLY CHRIST AT THE POINT OF ATTACK. Call upon Jesus, summon His assistance at the time and place that temptation occurs. Certain emotions can be awakened by a sound, a smell, a sight, or a word. These "triggers" must be avoided. Should they come upon you suddenly, call upon Jesus immediately. Christ will move heaven and earth to keep you from falling. You can stand in Jesus, you can fight in Jesus, you can win in Jesus. Bring Him into every facet and area of your life, even the smallest, seemingly insignificant ones.

STOPPING THE FALL

I have developed an ideology that I call "Key theology." I have averaged approximately twenty funerals a year from 1985 to 1991. I have seen a wide variety of responses to death. I have seen calm repose and wild, almost insane grief. I have witnessed men and women scream and shout and injure themselves. I have watched as a mother tucked into the coffin next to her dead son, a bottle of champagne, five hundred dollars in cash, a solid gold cross, and an Uzi machine gun (the real thing, not a replica). I thought that I really could tell a lot about an individual's Christianity by the way he behaved during a funeral. But of late I have changed my mind. I find that I can tell more about a person's Christianity by what he does when he loses his keys.

When someone loses his keys, what does he do? First, he begins to retrace his steps, trying to recall the last time he saw them. This is done mentally, closely followed by a physical search. The primary spot is investigated, followed by a secondary spot. Sometime before, during, and after this procedure, depending on the patience, temperament, and present disposition of the seeker, a mild annoyance sets in.

If after two spots are investigated, no keys are found, this annoyance increases to irritation. And if time is short, it quickly evolves into full-blown anger. In short, we get mad! Rarely would any of us stop to really enlist the assistance of Jesus via prayer. No! We just get mad. Anger works against us, of course, in that it tends to shut down the mind at the very time that we need our thoughts and memory processes opened up. So by our natural tendency to get angry, we are actually working against ourselves.

If we would stop to pray, we would do two vital things. We would enlist divine aid. Everything that touches us, touches Jesus, including something as seemingly small as lost keys. Second, the act of prayer is a calming, mind-freeing exercise that would allow us to step back from the situation and from the anger so that we could think clearly and remember where we left or last saw the elusive keys.

My thesis then, is that I can tell more about a person's Christianity by what he does when he loses his keys than when he loses his job or a spouse or a car or home. If a person is in the spiritual habit of going to Jesus first when he loses something as insignificant as a set of keys, then he will know how to find Him when he suffers a major loss such as a job or a husband or a wife or a home or a car.

If we have accustomed ourselves to run to Him during the rain showers, we will know where, how, and when to find Him when life throws its hurricanes, typhoons, and tornadoes at us. Everything that touches us, touches Him. That is a point that cannot be over-stressed. If we bring Him into the little things, He'll be there for the big ones. A classic Christian hymn intones: "Oh what peace we often forfeit/Oh what needless pain we bear/All because we do not carry/Everything to God in prayer." Why starve to death when there is food all around? Why suffer when peace is close at hand? Why be defeated when victory is within your grasp?

The average adult can walk from the bedroom to the bathroom of his own home without having to turn on the lights. This is certainly true in my case. I find that not turning on the lights allows me to get to sleep faster once I get back to bed. If you're like me, you can probably use the facilities, wash and dry your hands, and replace the towel—all in the dark. Why? The answer is simple: repetition. You've done it so often that the actions become routine, ingrained, automatic. It isn't a matter of brilliance or particularly adroit thinking; it is, to repeat, repetition! A habitual pattern, constantly reinforced so that no real thought is required.

That is the way it must be between us and Jesus. When a stimulus is perceived (trouble comes), the flight to Christ needs to be second nature. The path to His throne needs to be walked daily,

STOPPING THE FALL

particularly in the good times. Then when the hard times, the dark days, come, and we may not be able to see Him—when our eyesight is made dim by pain or sorrow or loss—we will be able to find our way to Christ in the darkness. We will be able to turn to Him without stumbling because we have walked that path so many times before. Turning to Christ has become habitual, ingrained, automatic—even with the light out. We can walk to Him blindfolded. I believe it is a little late to go about searching for Jesus in a storm. We must walk the path daily during the sunshine. We must wear a rut, as it were, to the throne of grace in the good times so that we can walk it blindfolded if need be.

In this world it is extremely easy to get lost, to be forgotten about, and to suffer in silence. We really don't seem to have time for those who cannot keep up. It is important to remember that Jesus never forgets anyone. He never met a person that He didn't love, and He has all the time in the world.

If the world, or even the church, has turned its back on us, disappointed us, and let us down, Jesus never will. He will be our closest, constant Friend. But more than that, He has a disciple out there who will help you bear your burdens. The church is not full of scribes and Pharisees and judgmental doctors of the law.

There are some wonderful, kind-hearted, caring Christians out there. It is true that the numbers are far less than they should be. It is true that some don't want to get involved and have no love to spare; and that far too many Christians are "polyester" convenience-oriented followers. Notwithstanding, there are some Christians as good and solid and pure as the finest gold. You must keep searching until you find one and hold to that one forever. If you can, marry such a Christian; if not, then keep that person as your closest friend and allow him or her to love you in Christ and to assist you in becoming whole in Him. Don't struggle alone. Don't fight in your own strength. Get help! Get Jesus! Never give up!

I Will Fear No Evil

CHAPTER EIGHT

The Land of No Regrets

In this closing chapter I want to return directly to the Word of God. The Bible has within its pages the answer for every situation. The principles to be found there will work for each of us if we apply them. There is, to be sure, a level of comfort and direction that can be gotten from studying the lives and experiences of others. But the truest and deepest understanding of the human condition is to be gotten from the Scriptures. How better to know about the working of an automobile than to consult the owner's manual? Likewise, in the Bible we are reading words inspired by the God who made us and who knows us better than we know ourselves. How better to understand the workings of our lives and hearts?

My burden is unchanged. It is to reveal the magnificently merciful way God deals with His children and to state again my understanding of God's all-encompassing love. Rarely are sermons preached from the book of Lamentations. It is a book of regrets.

We have often looked at heaven in a particular way. I should like to offer hope to you by looking at heaven from a slightly different perspective—as the Land of No Regrets.

THE LAND OF NO REGRETS

In 1974, a group of us college seniors traveled to Greensboro, North Carolina. We were a choir, and we were giving a concert at a church there. I remember the trip quite well for two distinct reasons. First, I recall it for the opportunity to meet and dialogue with the late Pastor Napoleon Smith, a venerable pioneer in the cause of Christ in the South. He was advanced in age, but his mind was sharp, and his speech was clear.

The second thing that brings this trip vividly to my memory is the copious amounts of food provided by Pastor Smith's wife. She was famous for her skill in the kitchen, and her ability to feed you until you waved the white napkin of surrender or cried "uncle" was legendary. Three of us were selected to stay with the Smiths during our weekend in Greensboro. As strong, robust college men, we determined that we would be equal to the challenge and eat everything that was put before us. Anyone who knows college men knows that they are always hungry. College kids, particularly males, are like locusts.

The quickest way to rid your refrigerator of all food—new, used, and leftover—is to invite a group of college kids home for dinner. If you really want to risk getting wiped out, ask them to spend the night. I will spare you the details of our battle with our hostess, but Mrs. Smith was better than legend. She fed us a staggering variety and quantity of food, followed by several desserts that proved conclusively that we were no match for her.

While we were recuperating, the other indelible memory of the weekend was fixed. It came as I spoke to Pastor Smith who, after well over sixty years of ministry, told me of his life's one regret.

About 1910 or 1911 Ellen White made a visit to the Oakwood Manual Training School, later to become Oakwood College. She wished, among other things, to meet with the students and answer questions. Smith, as a young Black man, didn't see why he should listen to a White woman. He reminded me of the racial climate in

I WILL FEAR NO EVIL

the South in the early 1900s—the distrust, the prejudice, the racism. On the day that Mrs. White came, just a few years before her death, he made it his business to be elsewhere. He told me of his regret in days to come—how His own bigotry had kept him from meeting and speaking to Ellen G. White, the inspired writer and co-founder of the Seventh-day Adventist Church.

Let us do a little experiment. Close your eyes and think about heaven. That's a difficult request isn't it? Why? Because when we speak about heaven we tend to describe it in terms of those things that won't be there. The Bible says that eyes have not seen nor ears heard what will be there! We've heard about the streets of gold and the gates of pearl and mansions bright and fair, but we don't know exactly what will be in heaven, so we are more comfortable listing those things that we understand won't be there.

There will be no more doctors or hospitals or sickness or death. No divorce, no fights, no gangs, no AIDS, or drugs, or diseases. No eyeglasses or canes or crutches or wheelchairs. No child abuse or crippled children. No television soap operas, talk shows, thefts, rent or mortgage payments (in fact the life we now live through Jesus is our mortgage payment). No crack, alcohol, or cancer. In short, most of the things that are a part of our world here will not be in heaven—including aging, turning gray or bald, and slowing down. For me, perhaps the most important truth is that in heaven there will be no regrets. Think of it, heaven is a land of no regrets!

In heaven there will be no regrets. Think about your life. How many of us have done something that we regret? We all have. Someone once asked the question—What if you went to church and instead of a sermon there was a video being shown? What if the title of the video was: Everything You've Done, Everything You've Said, Every Place You've Gone, Everyone You've Talked To, and Everything You've Thought Of For the Last Five Years? Would you have any regrets?

THE LAND OF NO REGRETS

We hear it so often—I regret what I said. I'm sorry that I didn't speak up. I'm sorry I went. I'm sorry that I did not go. I'm sorry that I made that decision. I'm sorry that I didn't make a decision. I'm sorry I waited so long. I'm sorry that I acted so hastily. Think about the times you've heard these things or said them yourself. But, praise God, there is a Land of No Regrets!

The second book written by Jeremiah might well be titled "Regrets." When Jeremiah, the weeping prophet, saw what God's people had brought upon themselves, he wrote the book called "Regrets." We know it as Lamentations. Serving Jesus consistently saves you from a lot of regrets, and the earlier you come to Him, the fewer regrets you have. For Israel, their cities were torn down, and their beloved temple destroyed; the women and children ravished and enslaved; the army slain and destroyed. The reason? Israel's refusal, their failure, to obey God.

Even in today's world, which eschews black-and-white absolutes, salvation is still a simple, pure thing. Obey and live; disobey and die. The Israelites knew why they were wasted, as we learn from Lamentations 1:16-18; 4:12, 13. God had pleaded with them for years, for hundreds of years. Justice delayed was assumed to be justice denied, and sin continued. They sought safety in diplomacy, signing treaties, making deals more than in God. Israel played the two great powers of the day against each other. By signing alternate pacts with Egypt and Babylon they sought to maintain sovereignty. They didn't realize that the imperialistic assertiveness of these nations was a warning from God. The Lord always sends warnings. Before the spiritual tires go flat, there are warnings. Usually the flat tire is a slow leak, and the tire gets progressively flat over a period of time with ample warning and opportunity for correction. Rarely is there a blowout—a sudden disaster. Blowouts do happen, but more commonly, spiritual breakdown results from warning signs unheeded and not responded to.

Salvation was not to be found in Egypt or Babylon, but in God—in a living, breathing, vibrant relationship with God. The fact that your name appears on a church record or that you are technically numbered among the people of God means little. We are really God's people only when we are walking with Him, keeping His commandments, living His love, walking as Jesus walked, and allowing Him to live out His life in and through us.

The Israelites ignored God's warnings and followed their own course. And for a while it worked. There were successes and reversals, but generally things worked. That is how sin is; it works for a while. Such is the insidious nature of sin. It is the reason that sin is so seductive, so enticing. It seems so harmless, so good, so enjoyable. For a while, husbands can cheat on their wives. The wives won't know—for a while.

Doctors and pilots can abuse drugs or alcohol and still operate on patients and fly planes, and everything is fine—for a while. Many skip daily devotions, prayer, and meditation, and things don't seem to change—for a while. One can even contract the HIV virus and function well—for a while.

But the Bible warns, "Be not deceived; God is not mocked" (Galatians 6:7). What is sown is reaped. Life is used up; abilities and life forces are squandered, and we are left with regrets. The taxes come due on your lifestyle, and you have nothing with which to pay them. You then see how Satan has tricked you. The yellow metal in your hand is fool's gold. And you are left with lamentations.

For those who love Bible history, the year 605 B.C. is important, as it is the date of the Battle of Carchemesh. It is arguably the pivotal battle in the shift of the balance of power from Egypt to Babylon as Pharaoh Necho's forces were deflected and Babylon gained the ascendancy. Israel, who had counted on her alliance with Egypt, had nowhere to run, and the words of the prophets came to

THE LAND OF NO REGRETS

pass. That which Israel never thought would happen, did, indeed, happen (see Lamentations 4:12).

No AIDS patient, no alcoholic, no drug addict ever expected that it would happen to him. That is the rallying cry of the damned: "I never thought." And yet in spite of all their turning away, God gave His people a promise of restoration. When you come to Jesus, the only regret you will have is that you didn't come sooner.

Think of what it would be to miss out on heaven—to live in this world of trial and trouble and woe, and then not make it to eternal life. Talk about regret! To be separated for all time from a Savior who has given all just to be with you. Talk about regret!

Let me close with this story. I am not sure of its origin. It concerns a young man who lived sometime in the nineteenth century. He was the son of a wealthy businessman who assumed that when his son became of age he would join the family business and take it over after his father's demise. The son, upon hearing of the great exploits of missionaries for Christ, determined early on to become a missionary himself.

Naturally, this did not sit well with his father. The simmering feud reached a climax in the son's second year of college when he dropped all of his business courses and began to study the Bible and preaching. The father immediately summoned him home and informed him that he would be cut off from all family support if he did not change. The son remained firm in his resolve and was dismissed by the father and cut off from all emotional and financial aid from home.

Having only the clothes on his back and a Bible, the young man was forced to quit school and work to support himself. He wrote in the flyleaf of his Bible two words: "No resources," and jotted down the date beside them.

The lad worked for years putting himself through school and working days and nights when and wherever he could get a job.

The regular four-year course of study stretched to eight because of his lack of funds. But finally he graduated from college. Sadly, he was now financially worse off than before since the school had consumed all the money he had earned and left him several thousand dollars in debt.

His parents came to his graduation. The father, in a moment of compassion, suggested that now would be a good time to let bygones be bygones and that he would pay his son's debts and give him a large endowment if he would reconsider and come back to the family business. The son's polite, but firm, refusal only enraged the father, who made it clear that he would have no further dealings with the young man. In the father's mind, he was no longer his son.

The graduate was unable to find a position in the mission field and was forced to get a job to pay his debts. On the first day of that employment he again wrote two words in his Bible—"No retreat"—and the date. He would not go back to his home or the family business. He would press on. He worked long and hard, too hard, in fact. He worked himself sick and was hospitalized. His parents were summoned since the doctors decided that he would not recover. His father and mother arrived several hours after he died. His only earthy possession—his Bible—lay on the table beside the hospital bed.

His mother took it up and carried it home. She was not allowed to grieve; the angered father refused to allow the son's name to be mentioned in the house. His Bible was placed on the table in the living room and lay undisturbed for a whole year.

On the anniversary of the young man's death, his mother was moved to look through her son's Bible. The father entered the room and saw his weeping wife; he grabbed up the Bible and flung it against the wall. Years of pent-up frustration spewed from his mouth as he gave vent to his disappointment. "Your son wouldn't come into the business," he screamed. "He wouldn't follow my wishes,

THE LAND OF NO REGRETS

my dreams. I had such plans for that boy—but no, he wanted to go to some God-forsaken country to be a missionary. But where is he now? Where, I ask you? With all of that work, he never got to be a missionary. He never even left this country. What a waste—what a colossal waste of life."

During this tirade, his wife walked over to retrieve the Bible, which had opened to the page on which the young man had made his notations. She showed the father what their son had written. The words stilled his voice and broke his heart. However, there were not two, but three sets of notes the son had written. The first, "No resources," written on the day the father had cut him off. The second, "No retreat," written eight years later, after his graduation from college. And one final notation, written on the last day of his life, only two words: "No regrets."

This young man never did fulfill his dream, but he had found Jesus. And it was Christ who sustained him when his family rejected him. It was Christ who gave him the strength to press on. And it was Christ who made the decision to allow him to rest from his labors. Do you not see the love of God? The only thing that matters in this world or the next is the all-encompassing love of the Savior. Go to Him; stand with Him; let Him be your Savior and Friend. You don't need to bring anything, for you have nothing of value—no resources. Do not hesitate; do not vacillate; do not procrastinate. Do it now—no retreat. He will receive you with open arms. He will give you a new life in exchange for your old one. And you will never be the same—No regrets.

Epilogue

Knowing, as I do, the mindset of many Christians, it has occurred to me that not a few will consume no small amount of time trying to ascertain the identity of the individuals spoken of in this book.

If that is all that readers of this book are moved to do, then they will do themselves and their God a great disservice. Who these women are, the actual names, is of little consequence. What they were is important. They were ordinary people who, when placed in extraordinary circumstances, summoned Jesus and fought back with the razor-sharp sword of faith. They have left a compelling legacy for us who travel the road to glory.

Rather than seeking to know them, seek to know Jesus. Not just the name, but the Man—the person. Work at developing an intimacy with Him. Seek the kind of relationship that will engender in you the level of faith that you will need to meet the trials that you will surely face. Your love will be tested; your faith will be tested; perhaps, even your sanity will be tested.

When you close this book, open your Bible and open up your heart and soul, so that when the winds of strife blow against your life, you, too, will be able to stand.

A Conversation With C.A. Murray

Q: You mention in the Preface that this book holds the distinction of being rejected by three notable publishing houses. How does it feel to finally get it published?

MURRAY: I knew I had something worth saying. I was so impressed by the women—who they were and what they were—I just knew someone could get something from it. Back in the early '80s I was doing a lot of AIDS funerals, and everyone was in shame and in secret, and I thought that a lot of them didn't have to be. And there were so many people in pain. I did 117 funerals, which is a lot. And it contrasted with the heavy sadness and terror that those people felt to run across these women and just see the total opposite presentation. It was just something that I had to chronicle.

It started with just Delissa's story, really. She was just so strong, and so upbeat, and such a nice person, that I really wrote what was just going to be an article for her, and then the other two came within a year. It happened boom, boom, boom. So that drove me to do their stories also.

Q: So it must feel good to be able to finally share these stories with a larger audience.

MURRAY: Yes. Those who read the stories, said, "It helped me. It gave me a different look at some things and helped me see that my problems were not as big as I thought."

Q: Life in New York—what has it taught you?

MURRAY: I think there is a particular edge to urban ministry. Sin is very close to you. Sadness is very close to you. It's right there in your face. You don't get a break from it. It's day; it's night; it's on the way home. I've driven down streets just as the police were putting the yellow tape around a dead body. So it's right there. Death is so immediate and so apparent and all around you. Every day you are immediately thankful for what God has done for you because He's keeping you; He's keeping you; He's keeping you. And you get a chance every day to really check your own Christian experience. You almost have to because you are faced with your own mortality so very, very often.

Q: *Is it tougher being a Christian in New York than say, Cedar Rapids, Iowa? Or Nampa, Idaho?*

MURRAY: [laughter] You know, the devil can dog you any place, but the stakes are so much higher here. There are so many illusions. Even on the way to church you're stepping over bodies or over drunk people. You've got 475,000 homeless people in this town. You've got 250,000 needle-using drug addicts. Every day young people are tested and tempted. There are drugs in school; there are guns in school. You know, it is tougher. What you have in Christ is tested every day on the way to work, on the way to the subway, down in the train, every single day. You never get any vacation from working on your relationship with the Lord. There's no day when you get to take a break. Because every day when you leave your house, there is something to test you. You're walking down the street, and some guy or some woman propositions you—I had an elder tell me how he stopped at a light and a prostitute came over and put her hand right between his legs. So every day what you are in Jesus is tested, you know. You don't get any days off.

A CONVERSATION WITH C.A. MURRAY

Q: OK, so here comes the next obvious question: Why do you choose to live and work there?

MURRAY: Because somebody's gotta be here. New York is a mission field. Some people go to Africa, and we call them front-line missionaries. At the General Conference, Adventist Frontier Missions had a booth, you know? And maybe we ought to have had a New York City booth, because it's a mission field. It's just as pagan, just as wild, and in some places as godless. I mean, you've got hundreds of thousands of "Christians" and churches on every single corner. But churches do not control this town. They're just another form of entertainment for a lot of people. Somebody's gotta be here.

And then to be honest, you get kinda accustomed to the pace. Now when I go to other places and the pace is a little slower, I get a little fatigued. But you get accustomed to the pace, and somebody's gotta do it. And you know, New York has never hurt me. I've had one car, two cars, three cars stolen—one I got back, two gone, but you learn to deal with it. And, like these three women, you find some people who are just so close to God and so wonderful in the midst of all this stuff that it encourages you to say, "Hey, we can pull some lillies out of the mud and the Lord can reach down into New York City and do some really great stuff."

Q: These stories don't have storybook endings—something publishers, including this one, hesitate to take a chance on. The feeling is, if it's not upbeat, it won't sell. Why did you insist on telling these stories anyway?

MURRAY: Because in my ministry I've met thousands of people who aren't living storybook lives. And if everybody in the books we read gets the pot of gold at the end of the rainbow, then those who know that's not going to be life for them, what kind of hope do they have on this side of glory? Who do they turn to? If everybody has the wonderful miracle, if everybody gets healed, for those who *aren't* getting healed, what is that saying to them? That the Lord doesn't love them? That their prayers are not heard? Some people aren't going to get that miracle, and there's got to be some hope for them too. And there's got to be some joy in knowing that even if my life is cut short now, the promise of God is still good for me. Not everybody gets the pot of gold. Some people do suffer as Christ suffered, but there is a reward for that suffering. There's some payback for that suffering, and if you hold on to Jesus, you may not get it all here, but you're guaranteed to get it all some day.

Q: You personally pastored the three women in this book. How hard was it to remain upbeat during their horrendous ordeals?

MURRAY: Suprisingly easy because they were by nature upbeat people. And that's another reason why I felt their stories had to be told. Because they endured all of this and remained so upbeat, particularly Delissa. She *never* had a bad word to say.

Tamara, she was younger. Things hit her a little harder, but she was a woman of great resolve, really great resolve. And the last one [Juliet] just would not allow herself to get down. All three of them in their own ways were incredibly strong people. Particularly Delissa. When I went to her house, you know, she's cleaning vomit, her husband's throwing bottles, and she's singing, she's humming. That kind of stuff, even if you went in with a little bit of a cloud, she blew it away because she just didn't allow sadness. She was content. And the other two

A CONVERSATION WITH C.A. MURRAY

also, they just didn't allow themselves to get down, and sometimes when I went in [to see them] I came out feeling pretty good because of the joy that they had.

Q: Even though you are a minister, do you often struggle with feelings of inadequacy in the face of such devastating circumstances?

MURRAY: Yes. When I came out of school, you know, you got your little B.A., and you figure with that comes, if not all the answers, 90 percent of the answers to life [laughs]. And then you run into stuff that's not in the textbook, that they didn't teach you in class. And these situations become a test of your faith. So many times you're left to question what you have in the Lord. Their struggle makes you question not only, "Could I do it as they did it?" but "Is my hold on Christ enough to keep me from spiraling down into this thing?" So yes, you feel inadequate a lot of the time.

Q: You preached 117 funerals—does it ever become unbearable? Just too depressing—all the hurt and loss? Does it ever seem that the gospel you preach is just overwhelmed by the real world's hurts that are ever present?

MURRAY: For me it was just the opposite. The only thing that makes any sense is the gospel. If it weren't for the gospel, you'd be in these same abject situations but without hope. Having Jesus keeps you sane in the presence of insane situations. I've seen this enough that those who don't have the Lord tend to act one way, and those who have a good, strong handle on the Lord tend to act another way. So the only thing that gets you through 117 funerals, or the death of a friend, or the death of a spouse, or the death of somebody you love is the fact that Christ is there. Instead of being overwhelmed by tragedy, it is the gospel that brings some sense and some sanity to all of that.

Q: You mention being disturbed by ministers who say things like: "What do AIDS and drugs have to do with Christians?" What bothers you about this?

MURRAY: It seems to say that if you are a Christian, nothing bad will ever happen to you. And there's a whole lot of Christians who know that isn't so. It's just a short-sighted statement, because there are some people who are innocent, to whom bad stuff happens. Sometimes bad stuff happens to good people, but God is still good, and that's when you've got to turn to Him. You know, you bank all this stuff with Him all these years, and sometimes you need to write some checks. You've got to draw on that account, if you've got something in there! At those times, that's when you've got to begin to make some withdrawals for your own safety and sanity.

Q: What's the main message you want your readers to get from this book?

MURRAY: Sometimes apparently bad things happen to good people, but even in the worst of situations God is still there. The Lord doesn't see death as we do. Death is just a detour on a road that's going to end in glory. And that even though your life may be cut short in death now, ultimately, it's just a little detour on a road that's going to reunite you with Christ. You're not alone. God is with you through it all, and if you just hold on, God will show you your Friend and Savior, and you'll make it ultimately even though it appears your life is being cut short.

A CONVERSATION WITH C.A. MURRAY

Q: What one piece of advice would you offer to readers who may be facing "valleys" in their own life or who may be called on to minister to those walking through a valley experience?

MURRAY: Though we get perhaps our clearest picture of Jesus on the mountain and we're feeling His presence, your relationship is forged in the valley. The ability to see and feel His presence is done in the valley. If you have anything in Christ, it comes out in the valley. That's the winepress of your experience. If you're in the valley (1) know that you're not there alone, there are other human beings going through those same valley experiences; and (2) there is in the valley with you a God who is right there, and that everything that touches you touches Him.

If you enjoyed this book, you'll enjoy these as well:

Beyond the Veil of Darkness
Esmie Branner. A heart-pounding account of the struggles, hardships, and courageous triumph of a young Christian woman who refused to deny her faith in Christ despite the physical and mental abuse of a Muslim husband.
0-8163-1713-5. US$9.99, Cdn$14.99.

I Will Die Free
Noble Alexander with *Kay D. Rizzo*. The stunning story of Noble Alexander, who spent 22 years in one of the most brutal prison systems on earth and refused to surrender his faith.
0-8163-1044-0. US$9.99, Cdn$14.99.

The Man Who Couldn't Be Killed
Stanley Maxwell. An unforgettable story of faith and miraculous deliverance in Communist China at the height of the Cultural Revolution.
0-8163-1235-4. Paperback. US$10.99, Cdn$16.49.

Order from your ABC by calling **1-800-765-6955**, or get online and shop our virtual store at
www.adventistbookcenter.com.
                      Read a chapter from your favorite book
                      Order online
                      Sign up for email notices on new products

Prices subject to change without notice.